Ultimate
SECRETS
REVEALED!

A CLOSER LOOK AT THE WEIRDEST, WILDEST FACTS ON EARTH

STEPHANIE WARREN DRIMMER

NATIONAL GEOGRAPHIC
WASHINGTON, D.C.

CONTENTS

CHAPTER 1

OUR WONDROUS WORLD

Nature is overgrown with secrets. Check the weather forecast, point a telescope up to space, or take a walk in the woods, and you're bound to discover hidden mysteries. Some might even be lurking right in your own backyard! This chapter holds the answers to some of Earth's biggest questions, from how to make a rainbow to what's hiding underneath Yellowstone National Park. Read on to uncover some of the best kept secrets on the planet.

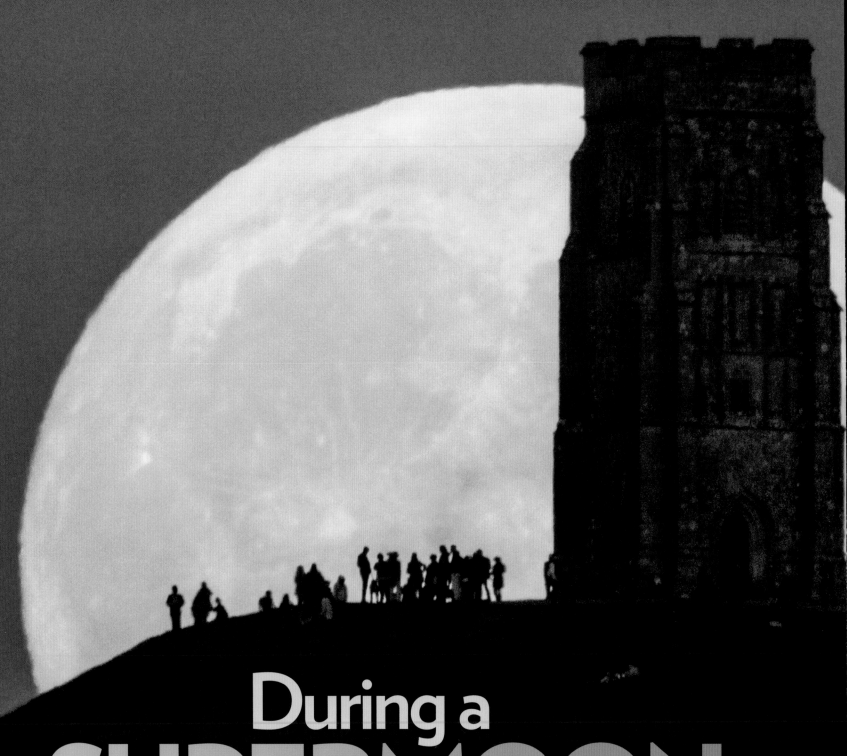

During a
SUPERMOON,
the moon appears up to
14 percent larger and
30 percent brighter
because it's unusually close to Earth.

WHAT'S THE SECRET BEHIND THE SUPERMOON?

You know the moon orbits, or moves around, the Earth. But did you know that the moon's orbit isn't in the shape of a circle? It's actually elliptical—more like an oval. So the moon's distance from the Earth varies as it travels its orbit. At its farthest point, the moon is about 252,724 miles (406,720 km) away from Earth. At its closest, it's about 221,441 miles (356,375 km) away. When the moon is at its closest point and also full, we call it a supermoon. This happens about once a year.

Supermoons are getting smaller. The moon is slowly moving away from Earth, at 1.5 inches (3.8 cm) each year. Superstition says that the supermoon causes everything from madness to flooding. But while there's zero evidence that this phenomenon has any effect on people's behavior, supermoons *can* actually change the oceans' tides. The pull of the moon's gravity causes the oceans to bulge out toward the moon, creating the changing tides. When the moon is extra close it pulls extra hard. But even a supermoon can only change the tides by less than one inch (2.5 cm). So the next time there's a supermoon, don't be scared to look skyward!

The moon may seem **bigger** when it's near the **horizon**, but it's actually an **optical illusion!**

HOT LIPS
(*Psychotria elata*)

If you're ever trudging through the tropical rain forests of Central and South America, don't be surprised if you see this bright red pout peeking out at you! Pollinators like hummingbirds and butterflies find the Hot Lips plant irresistible. And so do humans: The plant is a common Valentine's Day gift in Central America.

WACKIEST WILD FLOWERS

FLOWERS MAY BE BEAUTIFUL, BUT THERE'S NOTHING STRANGE ABOUT THEM ... OR IS THERE? YOU MAY THINK YOU KNOW YOUR BLOSSOMS, BUT CHANCES ARE YOU'VE NEVER SEEN THESE BIZARRE BLOOMS BEFORE.

FLY ORCHID
(*Ophrys insectifera*)

This flower might not win any beauty points, but it uses an ingenious pollination strategy. The fly-shaped blooms mimic the smell of a female fly, which brings male flies swarming in for a closer look. After landing on the flower, the flies take off, spreading the orchid's pollen. This tricky technique has helped the flower's range extend across Europe, from Ireland to the Ukraine.

MONKEY FACE ORCHID
(*Dracula simia*)

Mother Nature must have been monkeying around when she created this fantastic flower! These orchids, featuring flowers that look amazingly similar to miniature monkey faces, grow only in the cloud forests of Ecuador and Peru, at elevations between 3,280 and 6,562 feet (1,000–2,000 m). They weren't discovered in their hidden home until 1978.

PITCHER PLANT
(Nepenthaceae or Sarraceniaceae families)
Can a plant be scary? It can if you're an insect! The leaves of the pitcher plant grow into deep cavities. If an insect lands on the edge, it will slide down the slippery sides into the bottom, where it can't escape. Then, the plant digests it until nothing is left but insect goo. In areas with nutrient-poor soil, pitcher plants use this method to get nourishment. Smart, but creepy!

LIVING STONE
(*Lithops* genus)
In 1811, a man named John Burchell picked up a pebble from a stone-covered field—at least, he thought it was a pebble. The rock-shaped object turned out to be a plant! These "living stones" grow among real rocks in the South African desert.

SNAPDRAGON SEEDPOD
(*Antirrhinum* genus)
Snapdragons are common garden plants popular for their pretty flowers. But when the flowers die, they leave behind something shocking: a seedpod that looks like a human skull! It's no surprise that ancient people believed that planting snapdragons in their gardens would protect them from evil spells.

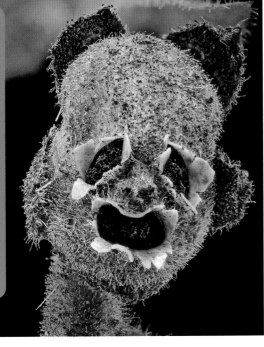

CORPSE FLOWER
(*Amorphophallus titanum*)
This plant might not look all that special. But if you're nearby when one blooms, hold your nose! One of the world's rarest—and definitely strangest—flowers, the corpse flower gives off a strong odor similar to rotting meat. The stinky smell attracts insects that eat dead animals, like flesh flies and dung beetles, which pollinate the funky flower.

TORNADO
Watch

>> Brave the whipping wind and look straight into the swirling vortex of the most violent weather event on Earth to discover the tricks behind twisters.

WEATHER WATCH

Tornadoes form when warm, moist air rises rapidly through cooler, drier air. As the air rises, it cools, and the water vapor condenses into clouds. If the conditions are just right, a funnel of rapidly rotating air will appear beneath the base of the thunderstorm, creating a tornado when it touches the ground.

SPIN CYCLE

As the air spirals around the central funnel, it can reach speeds of more than 300 miles an hour (483 km/h).

TWISTER TIME

The average tornado lasts for about 10 minutes, though some especially violent twisters have clocked in at over an hour.

GOING GREEN

Sometimes, the sky looks green just before a tornado strikes. That usually happens in late afternoon, and is caused by the angle of traveling light as it passes through the storm.

TWISTER TRACKER

Experts can now predict a tornado strike an average of 13 minutes before it hits, giving people in the danger zone enough time to get to safety. But storm-chasing scientists are working to improve this warning system beyond 13 minutes by getting up close and personal with tornadoes to predict their movements. They travel with laptops, GPS, anemometers for measuring wind, portable weather stations, and video equipment to capture what they find.

MEASURING A MONSTER

Tornadoes are ranked on the Enhanced Fujita scale, which judges the strength of a twister by how much damage it causes. The scale runs from EF0 to EF5. EF0s and EF1s can break tree branches. EF2s and EF3s can tear off roofs and walls of homes. EF4s and EF5s can completely destroy houses.

FLYING OBJECTS

Usually, tornadoes pick up things like tree branches, loose lawn ornaments, and maybe even buildings. But sometimes, the objects they carry are downright strange.

It's Raining Riches: Have you ever wished money would fall from the sky? It really happened to the residents of the Russian village of Meschera on June 16, 1940. Archaeologists think the source was an undiscovered treasure trove nearby that was scooped up by the storm.

Cloudy With a Chance of Tadpoles: When soldiers took cover from a heavy rainstorm near the French village of Lalain in 1794, they didn't know they were sheltering from more than just water. Toads and tadpoles began to rain down, landing on the men's hats and uniforms. The weirdest part? Falling fish and frogs are surprisingly common. This happens when a tornado formed over a lake—called a waterspout—picks up some passengers along with the water.

Free Golf Balls: What started out as a routine rainstorm on September 1, 1969, in Punta Gorda, Florida, U.S.A., became one for the history books when golf balls began raining from the sky. They piled up in the gutters, yards, and streets of Punta Gorda. The area is home to many golf courses, so meteorologists think a passing twister sucked up water from a pond filled with wayward balls and dumped it on the city. *Fore!*

ICE-COLD EXPERIMENT BECOMES RED-HOT MYSTERY

Scientists think asteroids and comets may have brought Earth's water from outer space.

In the 1960s, a student in Tanzania, Africa, was trying to make ice cream. Instead, he made a scientific discovery that still has experts stumped.

Erasto Mpemba and his classmates had a hobby of boiling milk and mixing it with sugar, then freezing it into ice cream. Usually, they would let the mixture cool before putting it in the freezer. But one day, Mpemba was too hungry to wait. He stuck his milk mixture in the freezer when it was still boiling. The whole class was surprised when his ice cream froze faster than his classmates' cold mixtures.

The discovery threw scientists for a loop, too. It's the water in ice cream that freezes. But how could hot water turn to ice faster than cold water, when cold water has a head start at reaching the freezing temperature? Decades of experiments didn't explain the phenomenon ... until 2017, when a group of researchers from Japan and the United States announced that they might have the answer.

Up to half the water on Earth is older than the sun, according to one study.

WEIRD WATER

Water is such an everyday substance that we don't give it too much thought. But it's actually the weirdest liquid on the planet. Here's one example: For most substances, the solid form is heavier than the liquid form. Burn a candle and the solid wax doesn't float on top of the liquid wax. But solid water—ice—does float on top of liquid water.

The researchers think that water's odd properties might explain the Mpemba effect. Water molecules cling to each other, creating what's called a chemical bond. In cold water, some of those bonds are strong, and some are weak. In order to freeze, the weak bonds first have to be broken. Then, the water molecules reorganize to form ice crystals. But hot water has fewer weak bonds. The researchers think this means it might be able to reorganize into ice faster.

HOT TOPIC

Many scientists still aren't convinced that the case of the freezing water has been cracked. In fact, some aren't sure the Mpemba effect is even real. Some scientists have been able to repeat Mpemba's experiment in their labs. But others say it doesn't work. For now, the mystery of Mpemba's ice cream is still unsolved.

A water molecule is made of a large oxygen atom (O) joined to two hydrogen atoms (H). When two water molecules get close together, a bond forms between them.

This bond gives water all kinds of weird qualities. In addition to the Mpemba effect, it also lets insects like water striders walk over its surface without falling in. Plants use it to pull water up from deep underground all the way to the tips of their leaves.

The world's largest CAVE is so BIG

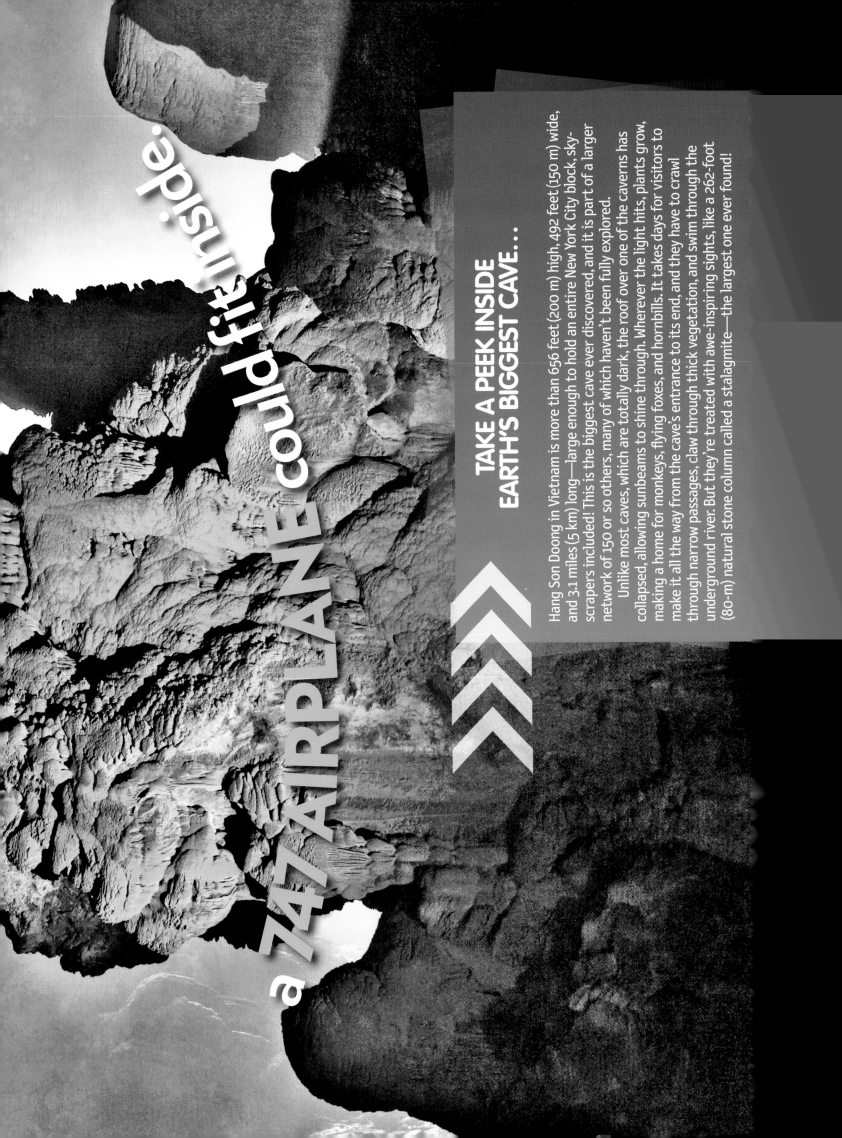

a 747 AIRPLANE could fit inside.

TAKE A PEEK INSIDE
EARTH'S BIGGEST CAVE...

Hang Son Doong in Vietnam is more than 656 feet (200 m) high, 492 feet (150 m) wide, and 3.1 miles (5 km) long—large enough to hold an entire New York City block, sky-scrapers included! This is the biggest cave ever discovered, and it is part of a larger network of 150 or so others, many of which haven't been fully explored.

Unlike most caves, which are totally dark, the roof over one of the caverns has collapsed, allowing sunbeams to shine through. Wherever the light hits, plants grow, making a home for monkeys, flying foxes, and hornbills. It takes days for visitors to make it all the way from the cave's entrance to its end, and they have to crawl through narrow passages, claw through thick vegetation, and swim through the underground river. But they're treated with awe-inspiring sights, like a 262-foot (80-m) natural stone column called a stalagmite—the largest one ever found!

What is a rainbow?

A rainbow may look like an arc, but it's actually a circle—the ground just gets in the way. If you want to see a full-circle rainbow, spray mist from a garden hose away from the sun. The rainbow circle will appear!

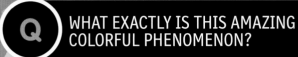
THE EXPERT: Raymond Lee, a meteorologist, or weather scientist, from the U.S. Naval Academy in Annapolis, Maryland, U.S.A.

White light enters a raindrop and bounces off the drop's back wall.

As the white light travels through the drop, it separates the light into many different colors.

Each rain droplet reflects all the colors of the rainbow, but only one color reaches your eye. It takes millions of raindrops to create a rainbow.

Q WHAT EXACTLY IS THIS AMAZING COLORFUL PHENOMENON?

A: A rainbow is what happens when sunlight passes through water droplets. When a beam of sunlight comes down to Earth, the light is white. But if the light hits raindrops at a certain angle, something strange happens: As the sunlight passes from the air into the water of the raindrop, the colors that make up white light are separated into red, orange, yellow, green, blue, indigo, and violet.

Most of the light passes through the raindrop. But a small portion of the light hits the rear wall of the raindrop. That part of the raindrop acts like a curved mirror. It reflects the light out to you. When this happens to thousands and thousands of raindrops together, they form a rainbow.

Q WHAT'S THE BEST WAY TO SEE A RAINBOW?

A: The ingredients for a rainbow are sunlight and rain. If you have those two things, there's a rainbow—sometimes it's just hard to see. The best way to spot it is to stand facing away from the sun. Put your hands out at arm's length. Splay your fingers and touch your thumbs together. Put one pinky over the shadow of your head. Then look at your other pinky—that's about where the rainbow should start.

Q WHY CAN'T YOU EVER GET CLOSE TO A RAINBOW?

A: A rainbow isn't an object; it's just a reflection of the sun. If you take a step toward the rainbow, your eye is in a new location. Now you're seeing the light from a different set of raindrops. So you carry the rainbow with you. No matter if you're walking at a snail's pace or speeding down the highway in a sports car, the rainbow will always move with you.

WORLD'S WEIRDEST PHENOMENA

OUR WACKY WORLD NEVER STOPS SURPRISING US! And new extraordinary discoveries constantly keep scientists on their toes. Discover the strange secrets behind five truly bizarre and out-of-this-world natural wonders.

VOLCANIC LIGHTNING

A volcano erupts, shooting a plume of fiery ash miles into the sky. It's a wonder of nature that would send anyone running for safety! But sometimes, nature doubles down on disasters: Bolts of lightning crackle *inside* the ash cloud! This bizarre occurrence is called volcanic lightning. Scientists think it happens when heat from the volcano gives ash particles an electric charge. When enough electricity is collected, the energy is released in the form of lightning. *ZAP!*

ICE BUBBLES

These bubbles underneath the icy surface of Lake Abraham in Alberta, Canada, may look frozen, but they're actually filled with flammable gas! Methane gas forms as dead leaves and other organic matter decompose at the bottom of the lake. Normally, the methane bubbles up to the surface and away into the air. But during the chilly winters, the gas can become trapped as the lake freezes. Don't get too close—popping one of these bubbles near an open flame can actually create a flaming fireball!

NORTHERN LIGHTS

Ancient people were shocked when they first saw the neon colors of the northern lights flickering high in the sky. They thought perhaps they were seeing dead souls on their way to the afterlife, the ghosts of their enemies, or maybe reflections of whales swimming across the sea. The northern lights, or aurora borealis, are created when magnetic fields on the sun send particles of superheated plasma shooting toward our planet. It takes the plasma 40 hours to travel the 93 million miles (150 million km) through space to reach us. When the plasma reaches Earth's atmosphere, it creates the colorful light show.

LAKE NATRON

This bright red lake in Tanzania, Africa, looks like the perfect place to take a swim. But don't get too close. The lake is extremely salty and full of sodium carbonate—the same chemical the ancient Egyptians used to mummify bodies. Certain bacteria thrive in these conditions. These bacteria are the favorite food of lesser flamingos, which flock to the lake by the millions to breed. Both the lake and the birds owe their pink hue to Lake Natron's bacteria. But even the flamingos have to be careful—they spend most of their time on islands in the lake, out of the water.

MOERAKI BOULDERS

Tourists visiting along New Zealand's Koekohe Beach coast stop short at this strange sight: enormous boulders the shape of nearly perfect spheres that litter the sand. Some of these rocks, called the Moeraki Boulders, measure nine feet (3 m) across! Scientists think they were formed nearly 60 million years ago, when marine mud hardened and was trapped in the cliffs that surround the beach. Millions of years of pounding waves wore away the rock surrounding them, leaving the hard stone spheres behind.

Heat-loving bacteria color the edges of Morning Glory Pool in Yellowstone National Park.

SECRETS of MORNING

Morning Glory Pool is one of the strangest sights in Yellowstone National Park. Looking like something that would be more at home on an alien planet, it's a bizarre rainbow of colors that shift from bright yellow at the edges to deep emerald green in the pool's deep center. Tourists flock here to marvel at the pool. But most of them don't know the strange secrets hiding below its waters.

Below the Surface

Yellowstone National Park spans 2.2 million acres (890,000 ha) of wilderness in the northwestern United States. Bison graze in green meadows and flowers dot the rolling hillsides. People come here to take in the peaceful scenery. But many have no idea what's under their feet.

Yellowstone sits on top of a supervolcano, estimated to be 37 miles (60 km) long and 18 miles (29 km) wide—bigger than the city of Los Angeles, California! Long ago, the giant volcano blew, leaving behind a crater more than 40 miles (64 km) wide. Scientists always knew Yellowstone's geography was odd, but until satellite photography was invented, they couldn't figure out why. They now know that nearly the entire park sits inside the supervolcano's crater.

Yellowstone's volcano is still going strong today. Heat from deep inside the Earth makes its way to the surface, powering the park's geysers and hot springs. One of these hot springs fills Morning Glory Pool. But what causes the pool's odd colors? That's what a team of scientists—including Joe Shaw, a professor of optical science at nearby Montana State University—wanted to find out in 2015.

Getting Warmer

Hot water from deep underground bubbles up through vents to fill Morning Glory Pool. "It's like a pan of water sitting on a stove," Shaw explains. "It's constantly being heated up from below." Shaw and his team used a thermal camera to take the pool's temperature, and found that it's a scalding 158°F (70°C). That might sound too hot for any living thing to take a soak in, but it's the ideal temperature for a certain type of heat-loving, bright yellow-colored microbe.

Shaw and his team think that the pool's shocking color comes from billions of these yellow microbes clinging together to form a huge mat. At the edges of the pool, there isn't much

In this photo from 1940, Morning Glory Pool appears clear blue, unlike its rainbow hue today.

Over the years, debris has clogged Morning Glory Pool. It was once made to artificially erupt and out came bottles, cans, $86.27 in pennies, 76 handkerchiefs, and even underwear!

GLORY POOL

water between the yellow microbe mat and the surface, making that part of the pool look yellow. But toward the pool's center, there is a lot of water between the microbes and the surface. As everyone who has ever played with paint knows, blue and yellow make green—the color of much of Morning Glory Pool.

Puzzling Past

The case wasn't cracked yet—Morning Glory Pool has another mystery. It's hiding in the pool's name. Morning glories are trumpet-shaped flowers that aren't yellow or green ... they're bright, sky blue. Why doesn't the pool match the flower it's named for?

The answer lies in the pool's past. Before the 1960s, Morning Glory Pool was hotter—about 172°F (78°C). But

over time, rocks have tumbled into the pool, along with coins and trash thrown by tourists. This debris clogged the vents that feed the pool, preventing hot water from flowing in. The more clogged the vents got, the more the temperature of the pool dropped. The yellow microbes that color Morning Glory Pool today couldn't have survived back then in those superheated conditions. To find out what the pool's color used to be, Shaw and his team created a computer model of the pool and dialed down the heat. The answer? Their model showed a clear blue pool, exactly the color of morning glory flowers. "Over the years, I've been visiting Morning Glory pool and wondering about the mystery of its colors many times," says Shaw. Mystery solved.

More than half the world's geysers are in Yellowstone National Park.

LIFE AT THE LIMITS

In 1965, husband-and-wife biologists Thomas and Louise Brock scooped up some water from Emerald Pool, another hot and colorful pond in Yellowstone. They peered at the water under a microscope and were shocked to see microbes wiggling around. They were the first to discover that life could survive at extreme temperatures. Today, scientists know that creatures called extremophiles can live almost anywhere, from inside rocks to beneath frozen sheets of ice.

Trees in Poland's
Crooked Forest
are mysteriously
BenT.

THIS IS ONE
CROOKED COLD CASE!

In a tiny corner of western Poland is the world's most eerie forest: the Krzywy Las, or Crooked Forest. Here, all the trees in one group grow in the same strange shape. Just inches above the ground, their trunks take a sharp 90-degree bend, then curve upward. Oddest of all, the crooked trees are surrounded by perfectly straight pine trees.

Experts estimate that the trees were planted in the 1930s and were between seven and ten years old when something happened to send them askew. There are tons of theories about what occurred, from a strange gravitational pull in the area to heavy snow that held the growing saplings sideways. But the most likely explanation is that local farmers bent the trees on purpose, to create curved wood pieces that would have been perfect for building the hulls of boats. The farmers likely abandoned ship on this plan in 1939, when World War II broke out. Eighty years later, the twisted trees are still growing.

All the curves point
in the same direction:
NORTH.

ASTONISHING ANIMALS

You might know that the cheetah is the fastest land animal on Earth and the blue whale is the biggest. But we share our planet with more creatures than even experts can keep track of, and each has their own claim to fame. Researchers estimate that about 8.7 million species slither, swim, and soar across Earth—but only about a million have actually been tallied so far. And with each new species scientists discover, new mysteries are revealed! Read on to uncover baffling behaviors and explore astonishing adaptations of the world's most curious creatures.

Caterpillars
LIQUEFY
as they turn into butterflies.

WHAT HAPPENS INSIDE A CHRYSALIS?

Here's the story you know: A caterpillar spends its time stuffing itself with leaves, until one day, it stops eating. It hangs upside down from a twig and spins a silky chrysalis around itself. After a while, it emerges as a beautiful butterfly.

But how does this amazing transformation, called metamorphosis, happen? The caterpillar actually digests itself! Once sealed inside its chrysalis, its body releases chemicals that dissolve its tissues, just like your stomach dissolves a hamburger. The caterpillar turns into caterpillar goo. The cells in this goo re-form to become the body of the new insect. Special cells instruct the ooze to form antennae, wings, eyes, and all the other parts of the adult butterfly. About two weeks after the caterpillar spins the chrysalis, a beautiful butterfly emerges, flutters its wings, and flaps away.

THE MYSTERY OF THE NARWHAL'S TUSK

Queen Elizabeth I once paid 10,000 pounds, the price of a castle at that time, for a six-foot (2-m)-long unicorn horn. At least, she thought it was a unicorn horn. The real source of the mystical headgear? A narwhal, a type of whale that lives in the chilly waters of the Arctic Ocean.

For centuries, people have been trying to figure out what these spotted unicorns of the sea use this enormous tusk for. Scientists had only theories—until video surfaced in 2017 that may have cracked the case once and for all.

TOOTH SLEUTHS

A narwhal's swordlike tusk first pokes from the jaw through the animal's upper lip when it's about three months old. "Over time the tusk can grow almost 10 feet (3 m) long," says Kristin Laidre, a marine biologist at the University of Washington. That's about half the length of the whale's body. (Try getting that tooth cleaned at the dentist!)

In 2014, a team of researchers, including Martin Nweeia (a dentist and marine biologist) who had been studying narwhals in the Arctic for 14 years, suggested that the tooth might be an enormous sense organ. He and his team discovered that the tusks are filled with sensitive nerves. The scientists think narwhals might use their tusks to detect information about their environment, like the temperature, pressure, or saltiness of the sea. The tusk could even act like an antenna that helps the narwhal navigate the Arctic Ocean.

But then, in 2017, the first hard evidence emerged. Using camera drones flying over the ocean in northeastern Canada, researchers captured never-before-seen behavior of the whales hunting. The video showed narwhals using their tusks to hit Arctic cod, stunning the fish and making them easier to snap up and eat.

TUSK TALK

The new video evidence revealed one way narwhals use their tusks—but it may not be the whole story. A tusk could be a multipurpose tool that also works as an ice pick, sensory organ, or weapon. And questions remain—if the tusks are so useful, why are males usually the only ones to grow them? For now, the narwhal's tusk still holds secrets to be solved. These unicorns of the sea may not be mythical, but they sure are mysterious.

Narwhals dive up to 4,000 feet (1.2 km) several times a day in search of halibut and squid.

Narwhals are social animals that live in groups and use clicks and squeals to communicate, like dolphins.

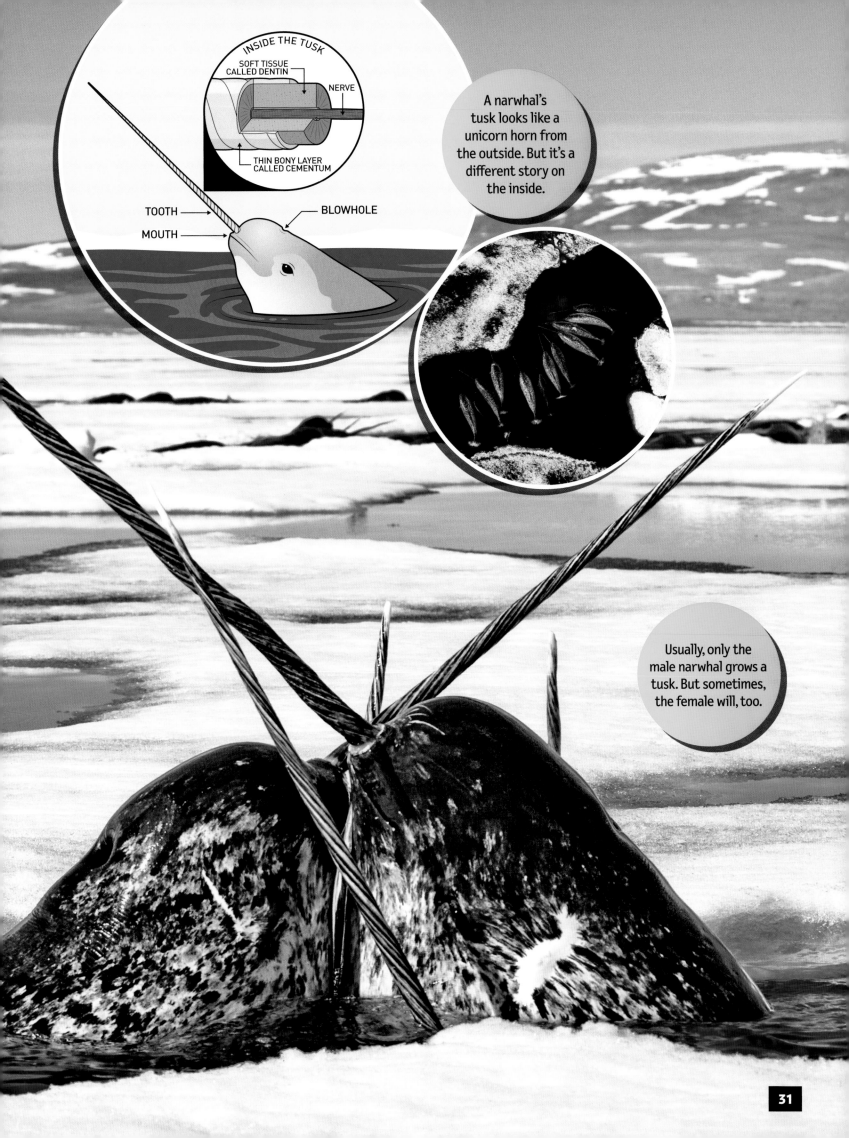

INSIDE THE TUSK

SOFT TISSUE
CALLED DENTIN

NERVE

THIN BONY LAYER
CALLED CEMENTUM

TOOTH

MOUTH

BLOWHOLE

A narwhal's tusk looks like a unicorn horn from the outside. But it's a different story on the inside.

Usually, only the male narwhal grows a tusk. But sometimes, the female will, too.

Odd OCTOPUS

They have slimy skin and curling limbs.

They lurk in the darkest corners of the deep ocean. Octopuses are among Earth's most mysterious creatures. Uncover eight of their most astonishing secrets—one for each arm!

CARIBBEAN REEF OCTOPUS

WONDERPUS OCTOPUS

MASTERS OF DISGUISE

By controlling special color-changing cells called chromatophores in their skin, octopuses can make themselves look exactly like a plant or rock on the seafloor. A single octopus can use as many as 50 different pattern disguises.

SUPER SUCKERS

Imagine if you could smell with your feet and taste with your hands! The suckers that cover an octopus's arms don't just grip: They're covered with chemoreceptors like the ones inside human noses and mouths. They're strong, too: Experts have calculated that a single large sucker can hold 35 pounds (16 kg). A common octopus has 240 of these natural suction cups on each limb—that's nearly 2,000 suckers combined.

INK ATTACK

If their camouflage doesn't protect them, octopuses have another strategy. They eject a thick cloud of blackish ink, then make a speedy escape before their attacker can figure out what's happening. Octopus ink also contains a compound called tyrosinase that irritates the predators' eyes and confuses their senses of smell and taste.

BLUE-RINGED OCTOPUS

NASTY BITE

All octopuses are venomous, but most don't pack enough poison to harm people. However, the bite of a blue-ringed octopus, found in the waters stretching from Japan to Australia, can be fatal.

STRANGE CIRCULATION

Octopuses have three hearts: two to pump blood through each of their two gills, and a third to send blood to their organs. It gets stranger: The blood these hearts pump is blue in color, from a special pigment called hemocyanin that helps keep the animals alive in the cold temperatures of the deep sea.

VEINED OCTOPUS

TIGHT SPOT

Unlike nearly all other animals on Earth, octopuses don't have a hard shell on the outside or a skeleton on the inside. That means they can squeeze into tiny spaces. Scientists once captured a video of a 600-pound (272-kg) day octopus slithering through a tube the size of a quarter! Engineers are trying to copy their body design to create "soft robots" that can mimic this maneuver.

SMART ARMS

Two-thirds of an octopus's brain cells aren't in its brain at all—they're in its arms. That gives octopus arms minds of their own: Even if one is severed, it will snatch up food floating by. By the way, losing an arm is no big deal—octopuses can regrow them.

VEINED OCTOPUS

BRAINIACS OF THE SEA

There are only a few animals on Earth smart enough to use tools. In 2009, scientists witnessed octopuses carrying coconut shells as they scooted along the seafloor. When a predator came along, the animals used the shells to build a makeshift hideout.

MARGINED OCTOPUS

SNAKE SURVIVOR

Opossums have a molecule in their blood that can neutralize snake venom, rendering it harmless. Scientists are studying the opossum in the hopes of creating a universal antivenom that could save humans from deadly snakebites.

ANIMAL SUPERPOWER SECRETS

SURE, SUPERMAN MAY BE FASTER THAN A SPEEDING BULLET, BUT HE'S GOT NOTHING ON THESE SUPERHEROES OF THE ANIMAL KINGDOM. READ ON TO DISCOVER BEASTS CAPABLE OF FEATS SO AMAZING, THEY SEEM ALMOST SUPERNATURAL.

COPY-BIRD

Like many other birds, male lyrebirds use their song to attract females. It's not unusual for a lyrebird to spend six hours a day calling. That's plenty of time for him to practice all kinds of sounds. Lyrebirds use their sophisticated vocal organ to perfectly mimic everything they hear: other birds, koalas, and even human-made sounds like car alarms, ringing phones, and chain saws.

SPEED EATER

This odd-looking animal, called the star-nosed mole, can find and gobble up food in an average of 227 milliseconds, or less than a quarter of a second. That's about the time it takes a baseball to travel from the pitcher's mound to home plate! The secret to the mole's speed eating is its strange snout, which is equipped with 22 tentacle-like feelers that the critter uses to feel around in the darkness underground for potential prey.

UNFREEZABLE FROG

When a human's skin freezes, the water is sucked out of our cells, causing them to collapse and die. But when a wood frog gets cold, special proteins in its blood pull the water out of its cells, then refill them with sugars. The frog's heart stops beating and its brain shuts down. But when temperatures warm, the frog thaws out. Water flows back into its cells, the frog's heart restarts, and the adaptable amphibian hops on.

RUNS ON WATER

Basilisk lizards never stray too far from water. That's because it's their secret escape route: If a predator gives chase, the lizard can sprint right across the water's surface to safety. The trick to this feat? Its feet! The lizard's rear feet have folds of skin that spread out. The lizard slaps its feet against the water, creating tiny air pockets that keep it from sinking.

REGROWS LIMBS

If a salamander loses a limb, it's no big deal; it just grows a replacement. Scientists aren't totally sure how they do it, but they know salamanders use special immune cells called macrophages. They're studying this salamander superpower to hopefully one day develop treatments to help humans heal from serious injuries.

Peacock
spiders
DANCE
to **attract** a mate.

THIS TINY DANCER HAS BIG MOVES!

Peacock spiders are only about the size of a pencil eraser, at 0.3 inch (7.6 mm). But for something so small, they've sure got swagger. When the male peacock spider finds a female, he raises his legs in the air, lifts his colorful rump high, vibrates his abdomen, and boogies back and forth. It may look like fun, but for the spider, dancing is a life-or-death business. If the watching female thinks her suitor is a bad dancer, she eats him! Usually, the flashiest males survive, encouraging the spider species to evolve even more showy colors and funky choreography.

Peacock spiders, which live in Australia, were first discovered in 1874. But because they're so small, no one paid them much attention until 2005, when biologist Jürgen Otto began taking up-close photos and videos of their spider sambas and posting the footage online. The tiny dancers became an Internet sensation. Today, scientists have found almost 50 species. Two new ones were discovered in 2015 and nicknamed Sparklemuffin and Skeletorus. With names like that, even spiders can be sweet!

Lyuba is the most perfectly preserved mammoth ever discovered.

SECRETS >>>> of the WOOLLY

When 10-year-old Kosta Khudi and his brother first saw the animal poking out of the snow, they thought it was sleeping. But the creature, a baby woolly mammoth, had been lying there for 40,000 years, frozen in the ice.

What had happened to the little mammoth so long ago? Scientists used modern technology to solve the mystery of the prehistoric creature's untimely death—and learned more about our planet's past.

Amazing Discovery
Related to today's elephants, woolly mammoths became extinct about 4,000 years ago. They ruled Earth while much of the planet was frozen in an ice age.

The baby mammoth, nicknamed Lyuba, showed scientists what these tusked giants looked like in life. "She's in as close to perfect condition as you can imagine," said mammoth expert Daniel Fisher. Little tufts of fur still line Lyuba's ears and ankles. Her trunk curls up slightly. And she has tiny milk tusks, which are baby teeth that grew before an adult mammoth's massive tusks formed.

High-Tech Detectives
Scientists wondered when this adorable baby lived and exactly how old she was when she died. Using a process called radiocarbon dating, the investigators examined the chemistry of her body. They found out that Lyuba was born about 40,000 years ago—the time period when the most woolly mammoths walked the Earth.

Lyuba's teeth held even bigger secrets. Scientists know that mammoth teeth grow in rings, like tree trunks. By looking at Lyuba's teeth through a high-powered microscope, scientists counted 30 rings that had formed on the baby's teeth since she was born. That told them that the baby was only 30 days old when she died.

Lyuba's CT scan shows researchers what a baby mammoth looks like inside.

Lyuba was found in northwestern Siberia.

Teeth helped scientists figure out the mammoth's age.

MAMMOTH

Frozen Evidence

Lyuba's body showed no signs of injury. So what had caused her death? Scientists put Lyuba in a machine called a CT scanner. A CT scanner takes a series of images, just like an x-ray machine. But then, a computer puts the images together to make a 3-D model of a body's insides.

When scientists looked at the 3-D scan of Lyuba, they discovered that her mouth, nostrils, and lungs were clogged with mud often found at the bottom of lakes. That's a big clue that she fell in, perhaps while trying to get a drink of water. When attempting to get free, she sucked in some mud and couldn't breathe.

Peek Into the Past

Lyuba's end was unlucky, but fortunate for the scientists who would study her thousands of years later. The mud protected the body from scavenging animals. Plus the lack of oxygen in the mud, along with the Arctic's freezing temperatures, kept the body from decomposing. These conditions were ideal to perfectly preserve the baby mammoth until her discovery.

After scientists had finished studying her, Lyuba went on display at museums around the world. Visitors peering at the little mammoth could imagine a world frozen in time, when Lyuba had walked at her mother's side across the Arctic steppes 40,000 years ago.

BACK FROM THE DEAD?

Bringing extinct animals back to life sounds like the stuff of science fiction. But woolly mammoths may walk the Earth again. In 2015, a geneticist named George Church copied genes from frozen woolly mammoths and inserted them into the DNA of an Asian elephant. The project is just beginning, but someday, Church hopes to build complete mammoth genes, then grow them into mighty mammoths.

Woodpeckers have two toes pointing forward and two backward. That keeps them from slipping down tree trunks. Spikes on their tails also help anchor them.

Woodpeckers have soft feathers around their nostrils that keep them from inhaling sawdust. They also have a special membrane that closes as the bird pecks, keeping out wayward wood chips.

Why don't woodpeckers get headaches?

THE EXPERT: Dr. Ivan Schwab, an ophthalmologist at the University of California, Davis, who studies woodpeckers as a hobby

Q WOODPECKERS BANG THEIR BEAKS INTO TREES AT 15 MILES AN HOUR (24 km/h), 20 TIMES A SECOND. WHAT WOULD HAPPEN IF A HUMAN TRIED TO DO WHAT A WOODPECKER DOES?

A: The way to think about it is, what kind of forces could your head put up with? Airplane test pilots can put up with about 140 times the force of gravity. They have to train to do that without blacking out. Woodpeckers put up with more than 1,000 times the force of gravity when they strike a tree—that's a little more than seven times what an untrained human can withstand!

A woodpecker's brain sits tightly inside its skull. But humans have fluid inside our skulls, and our brain floats on it like a boat. When we slam our heads against something, our brains bounce against our skulls, causing damage. If we tried to do what a woodpecker does, we'd be unconscious within a second or two.

Hyoid Bone
It wraps all the way around the skull, acting like a safety harness for the woodpecker's skull.

Q SO HOW DOES A WOODPECKER KEEP FROM PASSING OUT?

A: A woodpecker's head is like a natural shock absorber. First of all, their lower beaks poke out beyond their upper beaks. So when a woodpecker strikes a tree, most of the force goes to the lower beak. The force is then passed on to the base of the skull, down the neck muscles, and into the body—not the brain.

Then there's this special bone called the hyoid bone. In people, it's small and shaped like a horseshoe. But in woodpeckers, it's a large bone that begins in the upper beak, wraps all the way around the skull, and connects to the base of the tongue. This bone keeps the skull in place as the bird hammers away.

Of course, we can't say for sure that all this means woodpeckers don't get headaches. But if they did, they probably wouldn't keep banging on trees!

Brain
A woodpecker's brain fits tightly inside its skull, so it doesn't slam against the skull walls on impact.

Muscles
Thick, strong; they may help absorb energy as the bird drills into wood.

ANIMAL ZOMBIES

THINK ZOMBIES ARE NOTHING MORE THAN MADE-UP MONSTERS? THINK AGAIN. These real-life terrors of the animal kingdom use mind control to make their victims do their bidding. Ready to uncover their horrifying secrets?

ROACH CONTROL

The female jewel wasp hunts for cockroaches. But they're not her prey. They serve as living nurseries for her young.

First, the jewel wasp stings the cockroach and injects it with venom. The venom targets the part of the roach's brain that controls movement. The roach can still walk, but the venom destroys its free will. The insect can no longer decide when and where to move.

The jewel wasp grabs the roach by the antenna, like a dog on a leash. It leads the bigger bug to a burrow, where she lays her egg on the paralyzed roach. When her larvae hatch, the roach becomes their first meal.

FATAL FUNGUS

Fungus seems pretty harmless. But not *Ophiocordyceps*. This frightening fungus infects an ant, takes over its brain, and forces it to leave its colony. It then directs the ant to travel to a precise location in the forest: a leaf about nine inches (25 cm) off the ground and facing north-northwest. This spot has the perfect conditions for growing more *Ophiocordyceps*.

Helpless to resist the fungus controlling its brain, the ant bites onto the leaf, where it remains until it dies. Soon, a stalk begins to grow out of the back of the ant's head. The stalk rains down spores—baby fungi—onto the forest below. They find their way to new healthy ant hosts and infect them, too.

SPOOKY SPIDER

Female *Hymenoepimecis argyraphaga* wasps don't lay their eggs in nests. Instead, they look for an orb-weaving spider, then glue an egg to its body. Once the wormlike larva hatches out of the egg, it pokes holes in the spider and slurps up its blood.

A few weeks later, when the larva has grown to full size, its spider host does something strange: It rips down its old web and begins to build a new one. But this new creation looks nothing like a normal spiderweb. That's because it's not meant for the spider. Instead, it's perfectly designed to hold the cocoon of the wasp larva. After the spider is finished spinning, the larva kills it and eats it. Then the larva builds its cocoon in the center of the hijacked web, where it will stay safe and protected until it emerges as a wasp.

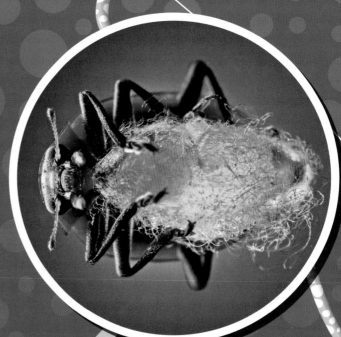

CREEPY CHILDCARE

When the female *Dinocampus coccinellae* wasp stings a ladybug, it's more than just painful—the sting inserts a wasp egg inside the unsuspecting ladybug. When the wasp larva hatches inside its hapless host, it's hungry. It begins to feed on the ladybug, eating its body from the inside out.

But the torment isn't over: When the wasp larva emerges, it spins a cocoon between the ladybug's legs and settles in. Amazingly, the awful act doesn't kill the ladybug, but she no longer has control of her body. She has become a living bodyguard for the wasp, twitching herself every now and then to throw off attacking predators. For the next week, the ladybug keeps her chilling charge safe in the cocoon until it turns into an adult wasp.

Looking at a **CUTE** baby animal

activates the same part of your brain as falling in LOVE.

>>>

SAY "AWW!"

Scientists have found that humans are drawn to animals that have facial features similar to a human baby's. If it has large eyes or chubby cheeks, we're squealing with delight. Big foreheads and round features leave us rolling on the floor with glee. When we see creatures with these features, our brain sends a chemical called dopamine through our body. Dopamine makes us experience the sensation of reward. It's the same chemical released when we eat a sugary treat, hit a home run, or fall in love.

But looking at baby animals may be more than just a fun way to procrastinate. A team of psychologists from Hiroshima University in Japan did an experiment. They had students play one round of a game that took lots of concentration. Then they had half the students look at pictures of puppies and kittens. On the second round, this group did much better than another group who didn't look at the babies. So looking at baby animal photos isn't just fun—it might help you think!

PUZZLES OF
THE PAST

Just because something happened long ago doesn't mean we have it all figured out. History holds all kinds of mysteries. As paleontologists dust off old dinosaur bones and archaeologists excavate beneath the sands of Egypt, they're discovering new information. Some of it answers questions experts have been wondering about for years. Other newfound facts just create brand-new mysteries. Turn the page and get ready to explore some of the past's most surprising secrets!

Ancient artists moved
more than 1,000

GIANT

STONE STATUES across Easter Island

The largest statue
weighed 82 tons (74 t)—
more than two fully loaded cement trucks.

STONE-COLD MYSTERY SOLVED?

These statues, called *moai*, were built at least 800 years ago by the early Rapa Nui people on Easter Island, in the South Pacific. Once carved, the stones had to be moved as far as 11 miles (18 km) from their quarry into place. The prehistoric people who built them had no metal tools or wheels. Their method was a mystery until 2012, when a group of researchers built a replica of one of the figures to crack the case.

The scientists showed that just 18 people with three strong ropes could have moved the giant statues. By splitting into teams, then pulling one team at a time, they could have "walked" the statues on their large, rounded bases with relative ease. Since the islanders didn't write down their technique, we can't be sure this is the true method, but it's the most likely answer so far. Maybe the old Easter Island legend—which says the statues walked into place—was telling the truth all along!

with no machines to help them.

FAMILY MATTERS

Lizards and turtles abandon their eggs after laying them, leaving their little ones to fend for themselves. So, for a long time, experts assumed dinos did, too. But the evidence proves that dinosaurs may have made great prehistoric parents. Scientists have discovered fossilized skeletons of mother dinosaurs crouching over their eggs, ancient footprints showing adults and babies walking side by side, and the remains of adults surrounded by young.

SECRETS OF THE DINOSAURS

DINOSAURS WERE COLD-BLOODED KILLERS THAT LOOKED LIKE BIG LIZARDS, RIGHT? WRONG. NEW EVIDENCE HAS CHANGED OUR UNDERSTANDING OF THESE CREATURES, WHICH RULED OUR PLANET FOR 135 MILLION YEARS. HERE ARE SOME SURPRISING SECRETS ABOUT THEM.

BOLD AND BRIGHT

For centuries, we could only wonder what color dinosaurs might have been. In 2010, one researcher finally cracked the mystery. Using a high-powered microscope, he discovered pigments preserved inside a 100-million-year-old dinosaur fossil. Decoded dinosaur color patterns revealed that some were actually quite flashy.

NOT SO SCALY

In 2016, a scientist was examining a chunk of amber at a market in Myanmar in southeast Asia when she saw there was something trapped inside. It was a 99-million-year-old dinosaur tail, and it was covered in feathers. Scientists now think it's likely that all dinosaurs sported feathers. But dinos probably couldn't fly; instead, they might have used their feathers to keep warm or to signal each other.

BRAINY BEASTS

Were dinosaurs really slow and stupid? A rock found on a beach in Sussex, England, in 2004 turned out to contain fossilized brain tissue from a plant-eating dinosaur that lived during the Cretaceous period, about 133 million years ago. Though small for its size, the brain's structure showed scientists that the dino was probably at least as intelligent as a modern crocodile. And crocs are no slouches in the smarts department: They've been spotted playing with floating objects and even using bait to catch prey.

DEATH BY DISASTER

Sixty-six million years ago, an asteroid the size of a mountain slammed into the Earth at 40,000 miles an hour (64,000 km/h). There was a fireball, then a 1,000-foot (305-m) tsunami and screaming winds. Red-hot debris pounded the Earth. But scientists now think dinosaurs didn't die instantly. After the impact, dust darkened the sky for two years. Temperatures dropped and plants shriveled up. With nothing to eat and no way to keep warm, the dinosaurs slowly perished. But many species survived, and without dinosaurs to eat them, mammals rose rapidly and evolved to become the species we recognize today.

When she was a kid, Earhart built a roller coaster in her backyard.

Earhart's flight across the Atlantic took nearly 15 hours.

Amelia Earhart flew 22,000 miles (35,406 km) on her around-the-world attempt. She was just about 4,000 miles (6,437 km) short of her final destination when she disappeared.

ARCTIC OCEAN

NORTH AMERICA

EUROPE

ASIA

ATLANTIC OCEAN

START
Oakland, California, U.S.

POSSIBLE CRASH SITE
Nikumaroro Island, Kiribati

AFRICA

PACIFIC OCEAN

SOUTH AMERICA

INDIAN OCEAN

AUSTRALIA

PACIFIC OCEAN

→ **Amelia Earhart's flight path**

ANTARCTICA

WHAT HAPPENED TO AMELIA EARHART?

Amelia Earhart knew she wanted to be a pilot from the time she went to her first air show at the age of 23. She became one of the first women ever to be a pilot, and the first female pilot to cross the Atlantic Ocean. But then she set her sights on a sky-high dream: She wanted to become the first person to circle the Earth around the Equator.

On July 2, 1927, Earhart and her navigator, Fred Noonan, took off to make history. They were never seen again. What happened to them is the greatest mystery in aviation.

LOST AT SEA

Earhart and Noonan planned to fly to Howland Island, a tiny, flat sliver of land just 1,600 feet (488 m) long and peeking 20 feet (6 m) above the waves. Most experts think the daring duo ran out of fuel while searching for the island and perished at sea. Others have a different theory—that Earhart and Noonan died not in a plane crash, but as castaways.

Amelia Earhart plans her around-the-world attempt with her navigator, Fred Noonan.

In 1940, a skeleton was discovered at nearby Nikumaroro Island. At the time, authorities thought it belonged to a man. But in 1998, researchers reexamined the records and concluded that the skeleton actually belonged to a woman about Earhart's size. While updating the information, they noticed something strange—the forearm bones were unusually long. Analysis of photos of Earhart matched her arms to the skeleton's.

Other evidence has been found on Nikumaroro: records of bonfires, bones of fish that the aviator might have eaten, a scrap of aluminum that looks like it came from her plane, and pieces of an old shoe that appears to be the same kind Earhart wore just before her disappearance.

MESSAGE MYSTERY

In August 2016, investigators announced that they had discovered red-hot evidence: documents showing that airlines received more than 100 distress calls between July 2 and July 6, after Earhart's plane crashed. They think these calls could only have come from Earhart, who must have lived for weeks or even months on the tiny deserted island in the middle of the ocean. The theory isn't airtight, but the team plans to keep investigating until they get to the bottom of history's most famous disappearance.

Weird WASHINGTON

> You know he was America's first president. But did you know that curly coiffure was his real hair ... and those pearly whites were fake? It turns out old George had a few secrets up his ruffled sleeves! Check out these facts about Washington that might surprise you.

DANCE MASTER

He might look stern in his presidential portraits, but George liked to have a good time. The first president himself described dancing as "so agreeable and innocent an amusement." And according to eyewitness accounts, Washington really could boogie down on the dance floor. One fellow partygoer gossiped that the Founding Father "danced upward of three hours without sitting down." Let's hope his wife, Martha, could keep up!

54

TOOTHY GRIN

It's commonly said that the Father of Our Country had wooden teeth. That's not true. But Washington did suffer from constant toothaches and dental distress. By the time he took office on April 30, 1789, poor George had only one tooth in his head. To make his smile more presidential, he wore dentures. They were made of human teeth, hippopotamus bone, and ivory from walruses and elephants, all attached with lead, gold wire, and brass screws.

HIGH RANKING

Nobody will ever rank higher than George Washington in the U.S. armed forces. When he died, the president was a lieutenant general. But as time passed, that ranking didn't seem to measure up to his accomplishments: He didn't just defeat the British Army; he was the father of the U.S. military, who established and organized the troops, shaping the way the military still operates today. So in 1976, he was promoted to General of the Armies of the United States, and it was decreed that no one would ever outrank him.

WIGGED OUT

In the 1700s, it was all the rage for men of status to wear powdered wigs (although the original trendsetter, French king Louis XIII, wore one because he was balding). Many assume George's hair was fake to match the trend. But his hair was his own, down to the pigtail and the perfect roll near his neck. It was also reddish brown, but he powdered it to make it white.

BATTLE OF THE BODY

Leading troops on the battlefield is tough enough. Imagine doing it while fighting a sore throat, hacking cough, and chills. George Washington suffered from so many illnesses that he's considered one of the sickest presidents in U.S. history. Diphtheria, tuberculosis, smallpox, dysentery, malaria, and pneumonia were just a few of the maladies that plagued him throughout his life.

GUARDIANS OF THE TOMB

SECRETS of the TERRA-

>>>>>

Some Chinese farmers were digging for water when they got the shock of their lives. A face stared up at them from the soil, eyes wide open, with features that looked almost human. But the face was not part of a skeleton; it was made of baked clay, called terra-cotta. And it led to the discovery of what many say is the eighth wonder of the ancient world.

Buried Treasure
Underneath the mysterious head lay a pit the size of two football fields. Inside it were thousands of life-size clay soldiers, hidden there for 2,200 years. Row upon row of the soldiers were placed in battle formation. And, remarkably, each soldier's face was different from the

next. "Every hair on the head and tread on the shoes is so realistic," says China expert Albert Dien.

After years of excavating, archaeologists found a total of four pits, some containing statues of horse-drawn chariots, cavalry soldiers on horseback, and high-ranking officers. One of the pits was empty and likely unfinished.

Telling Clues
Who could have built this huge underground army? The archaeologists had a hunch they knew the answer.

Found near Xi'an, which was China's capital city for nearly 2,000 years, the soldiers could be the work of only one person: China's first emperor, Qin Shi Huang Di (chin shure-hwong-dee).

The brilliant but brutal ruler was known for his big ideas and even bigger ego. He conquered nearby lands, creating the first unified China. He built the Great Wall, which still stands today. He also ordered workers to build a tall hill for his tomb. This giant grave—which is taller than the Statue of Liberty—was less than a mile (1.6 km) from the pits of terra-cotta warriors. "There had to be a connection," Dien says.

An Eternal Army
Ancient Chinese rulers were often buried with small figurines of soldiers meant to protect them in the afterlife. But Qin Shi Huang Di's terra-cotta soldiers were grander than anything ever seen. "The emperor had killed a lot of

Archaeologists have not yet excavated the final resting place of Emperor Qin Shi Huang Di. Opening the tomb could damage any treasures inside.

COTTA ARMY

people, so maybe he wanted a large army to protect him from his victims' ghosts," says Dien.

But it was the emperor's living enemies that took revenge—not the dead ones. In 206 B.C., a few years after Qin Shi Huang Di's death, invading armies set the pits' wooden support beams on fire. The roofs collapsed, burying the warriors and cracking every figure. The pits caved in more as time went on, and the soldiers were lost to the ages.

Since the farmers' discovery in 1974, experts have pieced a thousand soldiers back together. But some 6,000 figures are still buried. As work continues, who knows what other secrets these soldiers have yet to tell?

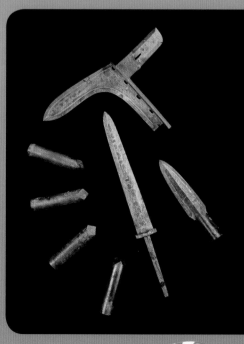

FAKE SOLDIERS, REAL WEAPONS

The terra-cotta army may not be able to do battle, but their bronze weapons could. The figures were found fully armed with tens of thousands of swords, axes, spears, lances, and crossbows. All were as well made as anything real Chinese soldiers carried into battle at the time. In 2012, experts analyzed 40,000 arrowheads from the site and learned that the weapons were likely mass-produced in multiple workshops where artisans crafted them under the guidance of a master craftsman.

Named *Titanoboa*, this fearsome constrictor was as long as a school bus at 43 feet (13 m)—the biggest snake ever discovered! *Titanoboa* was just one of many giant prehistoric animals, from the huge dinosaurs that lived during the Jurassic period to the elephant-size ground sloths that trudged across South America until about 10,000 years ago.

Why were some prehistoric animals so big?

THE EXPERT: David Polly is a paleontologist—a scientist who looks at fossils to study the history of life—at Indiana University in Bloomington, Indiana, U.S.A. He was one of the people who figured out what the *Titanoboa* fossil was.

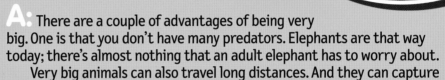

MAMENCHISAURUS

Q WHY WERE ANCIENT ANIMALS, SUCH AS *TITANOBOA*, SO LARGE?

A: There are a couple of advantages of being very big. One is that you don't have many predators. Elephants are that way today; there's almost nothing that an adult elephant has to worry about.

Very big animals can also travel long distances. And they can capture and eat very large prey—so they can go longer between meals.

Titanoboa mostly ate very large fish, and it might have also eaten crocodiles and ancient turtles that weighed 300 pounds (136 kg). Just like modern boa constrictors, *Titanoboa* would have wrapped its body around its prey and squeezed it to death.

Q SCARY! ARE THERE ANY DOWNSIDES TO BEING REALLY BIG?

A: It's not easy being enormous. One problem is gravity. The bigger you get, the more weight your skeleton and muscles have to carry. That's why an elephant's legs are like tree trunks. Elephants are pushing the limits for how big an animal can be, at least on land.

Another problem for reptiles like *Titanoboa* is that they're cold-blooded, which means they warm their body with the heat of the sun. A really big body takes a lot of heat to warm up!

Q HOW DID *TITANOBOA* SOLVE THESE PROBLEMS TO BECOME THE BIGGEST SNAKE THERE EVER WAS?

A: If you look at the biggest animals on Earth today, whales, they spend their lives in the ocean. The water supports their massive bodies. If a blue whale tried to spend time on land, its body would be crushed by its own weight! *Titanoboa* spent most of its time in shallow water, which helped support its weight and made it much easier to move.

And when *Titanoboa* was alive, the Earth was much warmer than it is now—where the giant snake lived, it was about 11 to 18°F (6 to 10°C) warmer than it is today. That extra heat made it possible for a giant cold-blooded creature like *Titanoboa* to warm its big body.

Q IS IT POSSIBLE THAT EARTH COULD HAVE HUGE ANIMALS AGAIN IN THE FUTURE?

A: Well, don't forget about elephants and whales! We do have some big animals alive today. But yes: Giant animals have come and gone through history. It would take a very long time, maybe tens or hundreds of millions of years, but more huge animals could definitely walk the Earth again. I certainly hope so!

TYRANNOSAURUS REX

SECRET CODES

DO YOU AND YOUR FRIENDS SHARE HIDDEN MESSAGES OR JOKES THAT ONLY YOU CAN UNDERSTAND? Then you're using steganography—just like an estimated 58 percent of U.S. teens. See how your secret code matches up to some of history's most famous.

LOST LANGUAGE

The Voynich manuscript is one of the most famous unsolved ciphers in the world. More than 600 years old, it's written in an unknown language that no one has been able to translate.

UNCRACKABLE

Kryptos, a sculpture built in 1990 outside the CIA building in Langley, Virginia, U.S.A., contains four coded messages—only three of which have been solved. According to the artist, once the remaining code is cracked, there's still one more riddle left!

CAESAR'S CIPHER

Julius Caesar, who ruled the Roman Empire as dictator from 49 B.C. until his assassination in 44 B.C., used a secret code to communicate with his generals. He swapped each letter for the one three spots later in the alphabet.

FREE SPEECH

The Underground Railroad was a network of people who helped slaves escape. They used a code to communicate, so if letters were intercepted—or slave owners overheard a conversation—they would not be caught. A "conductor" was a person who transported slaves; a "station" was a safe hiding place; "cargo" was escaped slaves; "Heaven" was the free country of Canada.

SECRET SMILE

There may be a real-life secret code painted in the "Mona Lisa," Leonardo da Vinci's famous painting of the mysterious smiling woman. Scientists have discovered hidden numbers and letters painted into her eyes.

Early Egyptians named their land Kemet, or "black land," for its rich river mud.

At 241 feet (73 m) long and 66 feet (20 m) high, the Sphinx is the largest statue on the planet.

HIDDEN IN THE SAND

SECRETS of the SPHINX

Imagine that you're an ancient Egyptian heading to the city of Giza for the first time. Your boat is racing along the Nile River when the pyramids appear ahead. These man-made mountains seem to stretch all the way to the sun! Crouching in front is their giant guardian: a statue of a lion with the head of a king. The Great Sphinx is as tall as the White House, with paws bigger than city buses. It's an incredible sight.

People have been visiting the Great Sphinx for thousands of years. But much about this mighty monument is still a mystery—including who built it.

Set in Stone

In ancient Egypt, people worshipped sphinxes as mythical creatures with the power to ward off evil. The Great Sphinx is Egypt's first large sculpture. Some think it was built as a protector of the pyramids, a burial place for Egyptian kings.

Nobody's sure when the Sphinx was built, but experts believe it was already ancient when Cleopatra saw it around 47 B.C. Since then, many other historical figures have visited the monument, from Napoleon to Barack Obama. But which historical figure *built* the monument?

Face Off

Historians disagree about who they think constructed the Sphinx. Their two top suspects are Pharaoh Khufu, who ruled Egypt from 2589 to 2566 B.C., and his son, Pharaoh Khafre, who reigned from 2558 to 2532 B.C. Most experts agree that one of these rulers oversaw the construction of the statue and had his own face carved atop the giant lion. But which one was it—Khufu or Khafre?

Some think the Sphinx is the work of Khufu. They say the statue's face matches a small sculpture of the king discovered in 1903.

In Egypt, camels are called ships of the desert. Like ships, they carry goods and people.

Archaeologists think the Sphinx was once painted with bright colors.

EGYPT

ATLANTIC OCEAN
EUROPE
ASIA
AFRICA
INDIAN OCEAN

Mediterranean Sea
ISRAEL
JORDAN
Sphinx
★ Cairo
SAUDI ARABIA
LIBYA
Nile River
EGYPT
Red Sea
SUDAN

But most experts, including Egyptologist Mark Lehner, think Khufu's son, Khafre, built the Sphinx. Lehner says evidence lies in a temple that sits in front of the statue. Workers built it after removing part of another structure that's been proven to be the work of Khafre. Lehner believes that this means the Sphinx and its temple must have been constructed after Khafre's first structure was built. "To me, that's strong evidence that the Sphinx couldn't have been Khufu's," Lehner says.

What Lies Beneath
Who built it isn't the Sphinx's only mystery. The biggest question about the structure used to be what was buried underneath it. One legend said the library of the lost city of Atlantis

was concealed below the statue. Archaeologists even went looking for it in 1926 and did discover a secret tunnel under the Sphinx—but it led nowhere. Experts think treasure hunters dug the tunnel long ago, searching for hidden riches.

But in 1999, Lehner found a different kind of lost city: a nearby ancient settlement that was larger than 10 football fields. Lehner believes it was home to as many as 2,000 workers who lived there some 4,500 years ago. They were not slaves, but seasonal workers who traveled from Egypt's farmland to build the pyramids in shifts. These workers likely hauled millions of stone blocks of many different kinds to build the pyramids, and chiseled the Sphinx out of limestone.

Disappearing Act
Today the ancient Egyptians' work is crumbling. Centuries of wind and water have ground away at the Sphinx's limestone, and shifting sands have threatened to cover much of it. The Sphinx's nose and beard are missing. Traces of pigment show it was once painted bright red, yellow, and blue. Pharaoh Ramses II began repair work on the giant sculpture more than 3,000 years ago. Modern archaeologists work tirelessly to repair damage to the sculpture.

By preserving the Sphinx, experts are also protecting clues that might still be hidden in the statue's stone. Someday, these could be the keys that unlock even more of the Sphinx's secrets.

KING TUT'S TOMB

As pharaohs go, Tutankhamun wasn't all that special. He was only 19 when he died after a brief nine-year rule. It's his grave that makes him the most famous of all the pharaohs of ancient Egypt. Discovered in 1922, it was found overflowing with treasures: golden statues, priceless jewels, an entire chariot—and even board games. Murals on the walls told the story of the boy king's funeral and journey to the afterlife. It took archaeologist Howard Carter 10 years to catalog everything. Today, the artifacts are on display at the Museum of Egyptian Antiquities in Cairo.

TREASURE TROVES

IMAGINE DIGGING A HOLE IN YOUR BACKYARD WHEN—*CLINK*—YOUR SHOVEL HITS SOMETHING METAL. AS YOU SCRAPE AWAY THE SOIL, YOU UNCOVER A GLIMMERING SURFACE. *COULD IT BE ... GOLD?*

FOR MOST OF US, THIS IS JUST A DAYDREAM, BUT EVERY NOW AND THEN, PEOPLE DO UNEARTH REAL TREASURE TROVES. SOME WERE SUNKEN IN SHIPWRECKS; OTHERS WERE BURIED BY OWNERS WHO NEVER MADE IT BACK TO RETRIEVE THEM. ALL ARE ASTONISHING FINDS.

TREASURE SHIP

In 1708, the Spanish galleon *San Jose* exploded during a sea battle with the British and sank. The ship was loaded down with 60 cannons and a stash of gold and silver coins and emeralds from Peru. When it was rediscovered in 2015, its treasure was estimated at $17 billion—making it the world's richest shipwreck ever.

STAFFORDSHIRE HOARD

One night in the seventh century, a group of soldiers stepped off the road near a small ridge, dug a pit, and buried their valuables. About 1,300 years later, treasure hunters with metal detectors stumbled on the spot. The hoard contained elite military swords and scabbards dating from the time of King Arthur.

JAVA SEA TROVE

In 2005, divers exploring the Java Sea, near Indonesia, found something more than fish and seaweed—they discovered a sunken ship. The vessel had been crossing the ocean laden down with treasure when it perished 1,000 years ago. The haul included nearly 14,000 pearls, 4,000 rubies, and 400 sapphires.

HOXNE HOARD

On November 16, 1992, a man was using a metal detector to find a hammer he had lost in his field in Suffolk, England. When the device registered a strong signal, he started digging—and discovered one of the largest stashes of Roman gold and silver ever found.

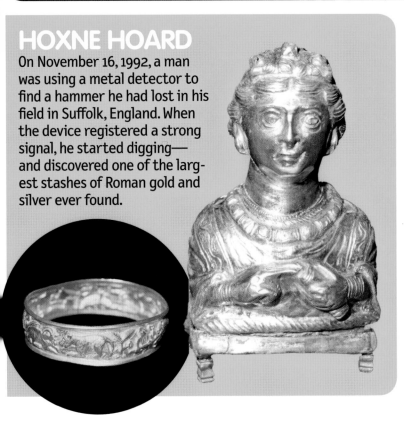

VIKING TREASURE

In 2007, hobby treasure hunters in North Yorkshire, England, happened upon a silver cup that had been lying undisturbed since 927. It was packed with the largest Viking treasure ever discovered: 617 silver coins, silver bars, and jewelry from as far away as North Africa and Russia.

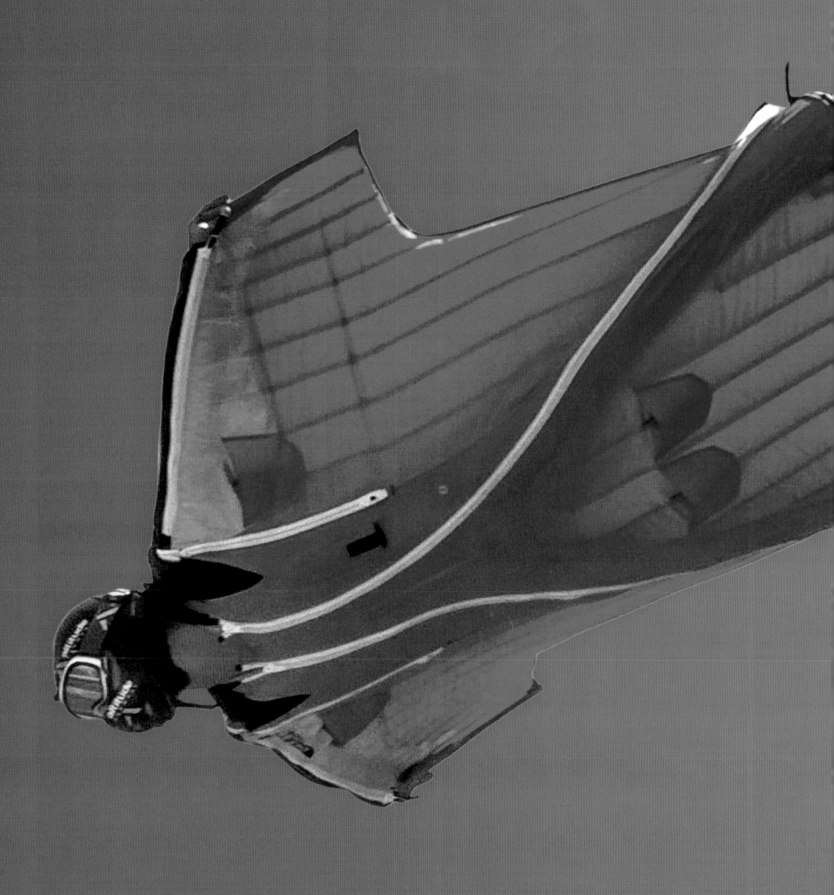

FEATS BEYOND
BELIEF

Every day, living things all across Earth teeter on tightropes, dive to the deepest depths, and even float through the air undetected. From dynamic daredevils and unbelievable illusionists to adventurous insects and other incredible animals, the record breakers in this chapter are amazing—but the secrets behind them are nearly unbelievable. Read on to peek behind the curtain of some of the most stunning stunts ever attempted.

Kinkajous can TWIST their hind feet backward.

YOU WON'T BELIEVE HOW THIS ODD ANIMAL BACKS OUT OF TROUBLE!

Their name means "honey bears"—but they're not bears. Their sharp canine teeth classify them as carnivores—but they eat mostly fruit. And they have monkey-like tails—but they're not primates.

So what *are* kinkajous? They're actually members of the procyonid family, a group that includes raccoons. These furry critters live in tropical forests from Mexico to Brazil and they sleep in tree holes during the day. If a kinkajou finds itself about to become dinner, it unleashes its secret getaway technique: It turns its hind feet around so that it can run just as easily backward as it can run forward. This amazing ability allows the kinkajou to quickly reverse direction to get away from its enemies' clutching claws. Cool trick!

Houdini sometimes hid a lock pick in his hair.

SECRETS >>>>> of the ILLUSIONIST

It was September 21, 1912, in Berlin, Germany, and master magician Harry Houdini was about to perform his greatest trick for the public for the first time. The stage was set with a sinister device called the Chinese Water Torture Cell. It looked like a huge aquarium with a strong steel frame.

Wearing a bathing suit, the magician lay down on the stage. Assistants locked his feet into wooden stocks. Ropes stretching to the ceiling lifted Houdini upward by his feet, until he was dangling above the tank. Finally, the magician was lowered headfirst into the water. Assistants locked his leg restraints in place on top of the tank with four heavy locks. Then they pulled curtains, hiding the trapped illusionist from view.

The audience leaned forward, holding its breath. Two minutes later, Houdini came out from behind the curtain. The lid was still on top of the tank, its locks in place.

How did he do it?

Clever Creator

Harry Houdini is known as history's premiere escape artist and illusionist. But few people know that the magician was also an inventor whose ingenious creations were the secret behind his most famous feats.

Houdini built clever tricks into his water torture cell. First, when he plunged into the tank, some of the water went splashing out. That left a small pocket of air at the top. Second, when the leg stocks were locked to the top of the tank, they loosened. Third, Houdini installed a hidden hinge on the stocks, turning them into a lid that could swing open on top of the tank.

Once the curtain was pulled, Houdini simply pulled his feet out of the widened holes. He flipped over and took a breath from the air pocket at the top. He then swung the stocks open, climbed out of the tank, and strolled out from behind the curtain, dripping but triumphant. The crowd went wild!

Escape Artist

In one of Houdini's first acts, the magician advertised that he could escape from any handcuffs that the audience or the local police could lock him up in. True to his word, Houdini freed himself from every pair of cuffs he encountered.

While performing for foreign heads of state, Houdini would do double-duty as a spy, then turn over information he learned to the British Secret Service.

Houdini had trick handcuffs that would snap open when turned upside down.

HOUDINI

His performance impressed a theater manager, who gave the young illusionist his first big break onstage.

To perform this seemingly impossible feat, Houdini had to study hard. He spent his entire life learning about handcuffs, and probably knew more about how they worked than anyone else on Earth. Houdini would study the cuffs, then hide the right key on his body—often in his mouth. Later on, he got help from a hidden device: a steel belt he'd invented that could be rotated with a flick of his elbow. The belt was outfitted with compartments full of keys and lock picks. Houdini would simply spin the belt until he found the tool he needed. A little fiddling and—*presto!*—he was free.

Tricks of the Trade

Unlike modern magicians, Houdini didn't have tools like technology and special effects. But nearly a century after his death, his feats still seem ... well, magical. His incredible illusions—and the tricks behind him—stand the test of time. Inventions he left behind reveal some of his secrets, like hidden blades he used to slice ropes and secret escape panels he shimmied through. But many of his tricks are still waiting to be cracked. On January 7, 1918, Houdini performed one of his most famous feats ever: He led an elephant into a large cabinet ... and then it disappeared. The cabinet was lost, and to this day, how Houdini hoodwinked the crowd remains a mystery.

HOW TO ESCAPE FROM A STRAITJACKET

Some of Houdini's illusions didn't involve tools or inventions, just smart thinking and a lot of practice. In his Hanging Straitjacket Escape, Houdini used a series of smart moves to make sure there was enough slack in the jacket for him to wiggle free.

He crossed his arms over his chest with his stronger right arm on the outside, tensing his muscles. (Houdini bulked up just for this reason.) As the jacket was pulled around the back, Houdini pushed outward to loosen the material at his chest. As it was buckled, he took in a huge breath, expanding his chest.

Once he was upside down, suspended in the air, Houdini would pull his right arm over his head. His upside-down position gave him a little boost from gravity. Then he used his teeth to unbuckle his straps and wiggle out of the straitjacket. If he got stuck, the illusionist could dislocate his shoulder to free his arm. Ouch!

EXTREME SPORTS

SOCCER, BASKETBALL, FOOTBALL, BASEBALL, RUGBY ... whatever the sport, almost every one requires athletes to push themselves to the limit and perform some fantastic feats to get the win. But if you think that's extreme, get a load of these unbelievable athletes.

WINGSUIT FLYING

It's been called the world's most dangerous sport. In wingsuit flying, brave participants zip into a suit that makes them look like flying squirrels, then jump out of planes, off cliffs, or sometimes from the top of skyscrapers. Fliers zoom at speeds of up to 150 miles per hour (241 km/h) before snapping open a parachute and floating safely to the ground.

STREET LUGE

This speeding sport first appeared in Southern California, U.S.A., when skateboarders looking for a thrill flopped onto their boards belly first and went hurtling down steep roads. Today, street luge is an official sport with an annual world championship, special boards, and full-body suits to prevent a wicked case of road rash. Participants zip down roads just millimeters above the pavement, reaching speeds of nearly 100 miles an hour (161 km/h).

OSTRICH RIDING

It might seem too odd to be true. But in parts of Africa, ostrich racing is a real sport! Riders mount up on their feathered steeds and compete to see who can reach the finish line first. If you're still skeptical, consider this: Ostriches can travel at up to 27 miles an hour (43 km/h) and cover 16 feet (5 m) in a single stride. The sport is nothing new: Historians have uncovered a statue of ancient Egyptian queen Arsinoe II aboard an ostrich!

CREEKING

For those who consider white-water rafting too tame, there's another—highly dangerous—sport to try. In this wild water activity, participants paddle their kayaks straight off waterfalls! Warning: experts only. Creekers have been known to get jammed between rocks, stuck underwater, or even have their kayaks break underneath them!

ZORBING

If you've ever watched a hamster rolling in a plastic ball and thought, "That looks fun," zorbing might be the activity for you. In this strange sport, participants climb into giant inflatable balls called Zorbs, then roll and bounce their way down hills. Once zorbers have mastered the basics, they can even participate in spin-off sports like Bubble Football and Snow Bowling.

INVISIBLE
Aircraft

» **Throughout the ages, secrecy has always been a supreme battle strategy.**

Today's tactics are no different, especially when you look to the skies. Stealth aircraft are engineered to avoid detection with sophisticated technology. Here's how these unbelievable flying objects pull a disappearing act.

DETECTING DEVICE

Here's how most planes are spotted: A radar transmitter sends out bursts of energy in the form of radio waves. If there's an object in the sky, the signal will reflect off its surface and bounce back to the receiver. The object shows up as a dot on a screen.

TAILLESS DESIGN

Most planes have a vertical tail, but that reflects radar signals right back to the receiver that's looking for them. Some stealth planes, like the B-2, do away with the tail. That makes them more unstable, but it's worth it for the sneak factor.

ALL ABOUT THE ANGLES

Most airplanes have rounded edges. That makes them better at flying, but it's also the perfect radar reflector, because the round shape means that no matter where the signal hits, some of it gets reflected back to the receiver. Unlike a regular airplane, a stealth aircraft is made of flat surfaces. When a radar signal hits the plane, it bounces away.

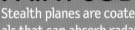

PAINT JOB

Stealth planes are coated with materials that can absorb radar. Many are painted with a special substance that contains tiny bits of iron. (That gives them their black color.) The iron absorbs the radar signal, so instead of bouncing back, the signal converts into heat and fizzles away.

HIDDEN ENGINES

An aircraft's engines are highly reflective. In a regular commercial plane, engines are located on the wings. But in a stealth plane, they're hidden inside the body of the aircraft where radar can't see them. A stealth plane's engines are also incredibly powerful: SR-71 Blackbird engines have enough power to propel an ocean liner!

LIKE A BIRD

All these stealth tactics together make for one hard-to-spot plane. The B-2 has a 170-foot (52-m) wingspan ... but on a radar screen, the flying object appears no bigger than a bird. Nothing to see here!

FUELING UP

You can't just stop and gas up in the middle of a stealth mission. When a B-2 stealth aircraft is running on empty, a panel opens on top of the craft. Another plane pumps fuel through the port—while in midair! With one refueling, a B-2 can fly almost halfway around the globe.

DECODING DRAGONFLIES

Dragonflies are the stunt fliers of the insect world. These airborne acrobats can zoom in bursts of speed up to 60 miles an hour (97 km/h). They can journey thousands of miles across oceans and turn so tightly they generate a force nine times stronger than gravity.

Why all the airborne antics? Dragonflies feast on other fast fliers, such as flies, mosquitoes, and gnats, nabbing them right out of thin air. How do they outmaneuver other insects to become some of the most sophisticated flying machines on Earth?

FEATS OF FLIGHT

Measuring a dragonfly's moves "is not easy," says Anthony Leonardo, a neuroscientist at Howard Hughes Medical Institute's Janelia Farm Research Campus in Ashburn, Virginia, U.S.A. That's because the real action is going on inside the dragonfly's flight control center—its brain.

Leonardo and his team built a tiny backpack that a dragonfly could wear in flight. It weighed just .0014 ounce (40 mg)—that's as much as a few grains of sand. Electrodes connected to the dragonfly's brain cells used for steering could record exactly what was going on while the insect was airborne.

Dragonflies catch their prey 95 percent of the time. Compare that to a lion's success rate: just 30 percent!

The scientists tried to get the dragonflies to hunt in their lab, but the insects were a little shy. So the team built them a habitat complete with a fake-grass floor, a small pond, and a wall mural to make the room look like a meadow. Then they released some tasty fruit flies. Eighteen high-speed cameras watched what happened next.

THINKING AHEAD

What the researchers discovered surprised them. "We used to think dragonflies hunted exclusively by reacting to the movements of their prey," says Leonardo. Instead, the scientists found that dragonflies chase down insects mainly by predicting the flight path of their target.

As it flies, a dragonfly's head is constantly rotating to track where its prey is. But its body flies to where the prey is going. "He's looking right at the prey, but he's flying to where it will be in the future," says Leonardo.

Next, Leonardo and his team hope to map the brain cells that guide a dragonfly's maneuvers. That could help them learn how the human brain makes predictions—everything from which direction you should run to catch a baseball to which topics you think might be on your history test.

The backpack that researchers created to study dragonflies has tiny wires connecting to the insect's neurons. The backpack then broadcasts information to the scientists.

Prehistoric dragonflies with wings two feet (0.6 m) wide once flew the skies.

Dragonflies can chase down and eat 100 flies per day.

HIGH-WIRE
Stunt

He pushes his foot over the ledge, feeling a thin, steel cable with his toes. Does he step forward into the void? You might think he's saying, "No way!" but professional tightrope walkers do it for a living. These are the secrets that keep them sky-high.

SLIP GRIP

The steel cable tightrope walkers balance on isn't just thin—it also tends to rotate as they walk across it. To stay on the wire, tightrope walkers have to fight this spinning force.

BALANCE BEAM

If you've ever walked on a balance beam, you know the best way to keep from toppling is to hold your arms out. That's because if you start to slip, you can counterbalance with your arms to correct your position and stay stable. Many tightrope walkers take this one step further by carrying a long pole. The ends of the pole bend down, helping lower their center of gravity.

SWEET SPOT

If there's too much slack in the wire, it swings back and forth under the walker's feet. But if the rope is too tight, it vibrates quickly. In between is a sweet spot where the amount of swing is easiest to ride out—about three feet (1 m) of sag.

TOP TIGHTROPE RECORDS

First tightrope walk over Niagara Falls: Charles Blondin of France tottered 1,100 feet (335 m) across the roaring Niagara Falls on June 30, 1859. After that, he repeated the feat blindfolded, on stilts, pushing a wheelbarrow, and pausing halfway to make an omelet. Show off!

Fastest motorcycle wheelie on a tightrope: Johann Traber of Germany zoomed into this record at 33 miles an hour (53 km/h).

Highest 8-person tightrope pyramid: The Flying Wallendas made history when they formed a pyramid suspended 25 feet (7.6 m) up on February 20, 2001.

Most spins on a tightrope in two minutes: Maimaitiaili Abula of China set this dizzying record: 41 spins on September 20, 2007.

Greatest distance: In the highest of all high-wire achievements, Bello Nock of the U.S. walked 429 feet (130 m), longer than a football field, on a wire attached to poles atop a cruise ship on November 10, 2010.

STAND TALL, STAY LOW

Tightrope walkers keep a straight back and bend their knees. This brings their weight closer to the wire. The goal is to keep a low center of gravity. Think about pushing over a vase—what shape is easier to knock down, a tall skinny one or a short wide one? Short and wide is more stable, because most of the mass is close to the ground.

Minerals in the rising water harden into chimneys. These chimneys can be very tall—one off the coast of Oregon, U.S.A., reached the height of a 15-story building!

Deep-sea vent animals live in water more acidic than vinegar.

Under the seafloor, cold seawater mixes with hot magma and rises through the vents.

How can creatures survive at the bottom of the ocean?

THE EXPERT: Santiago Herrera, a deep-sea oceanographer at Lehigh University in Pennsylvania, U.S.A.

Q HOW DID WE DISCOVER LIFE IN THE DEEP SEA?

A: In 1977, scientists were investigating the ocean floor with the submarine *Alvin* when they stumbled upon a hydrothermal vent—which is kind of like a pipe that releases heat from deep inside the Earth. The water spewing from these vents can be over 700°F (371°C), and it's full of chemicals like hydrogen sulfide that are extremely toxic to most life-forms. So the researchers were shocked by what they saw: huge communities of animals crawling all over the vents.

They saw giant tube worms nine feet (3 m) long. They saw huge clams, mussels, and crabs. Today, scientists have discovered hundreds of species that live happily at hydrothermal vents.

Since vent animals were first discovered in 1977, scientists have discovered a new species, like this yeti crab, about every 10 days.

Q HOW DO MOST ANIMALS ON EARTH GET THEIR ENERGY?

A: From the sun. Plants capture the sun's energy and store it. Animals eat those plants, and then predators eat those animals. That's how energy spreads along the food web.

Until the discovery of these hydrothermal vent animals, we thought that only a little energy reached the bottom of the ocean floor. The scraps of other animals' meals sometimes sink to the sea-floor. But by the time they get there, almost all the edible parts are gone. Very few animals are able to survive on these bits of food. That is the only kind of deep-sea life we thought was possible.

Q HOW DO HYDROTHERMAL VENT ANIMALS GET THEIR ENERGY?

A: It doesn't come from the sun: It comes from inside the Earth. Some bacteria can break down the chemicals in the vent water, like hydrogen and hydrogen sulfide, and capture the energy. They play the same role as plants everywhere else on Earth.

Some hydrothermal vent animals eat these bacteria, like cows grazing on grass. Predators like fish eat those grazers. Other animals, like tube worms, actually make the bacteria a part of their bodies. A tube worm doesn't have a digestive system—instead, it has a long bag filled with bacteria. Tube worms give the bacteria a place to live, and in return, the bacteria make their meals.

UNDERSEA PREDATORS

IF YOU GET A HANKERING FOR A SNACK, YOU CAN JUST GO TO THE KITCHEN AND MAKE YOURSELF A SANDWICH. But animals don't have it so easy. Wild PB&Js don't exactly roam the forest. These bizarre predators come with some clever hunting strategies. Here are their secrets:

KILLER BUBBLES

When all you eat is tiny fish, it takes a lot of work to get a full meal—especially if you're the size of a school bus! That's why giant humpback whales came up with a smart strategy for catching more fish at once. These underwater acrobats swim in a spiral pattern while blowing a string of bubbles out their blowholes. The fish are corralled into a tight group for easy eating.

SEAL SMACK

A killer whale made headlines when it was caught on camera smacking a seal 80 feet (42 m) into the air with its tail. But it turns out this wasn't just an oddly annoyed orca. Scientists say that many marine animals, like seals, have sharp claws that can injure whales. To keep from getting hurt, orcas use their tails to punt attackers as far away as possible.

FISHING LURE

Fishing takes skill. And the frogfish is a master fisherman. It settles into the coral reef, its warty skin blending in with the coral around it. Then, the frogfish extends its lure: a built-in fishing pole with what looks like a shrimp, worm, or small fish dangling on the end. It waits for a curious fish to swim close, then—*CHOMP!*

KNOCKOUT PUNCH

Though they're just inches long, mantis shrimp can throw the fastest punch in the animal kingdom. The punch's power comes from the shrimp's hinged arm. When the creature wants to attack, it locks its arm in place, then contracts its muscles, building up energy. When it releases the arm—*SNAP!*—the strike is as fast as a rifle bullet. Mantis shrimp have even been known to shatter their aquarium glass with a single punch.

SHOCKING STRATEGY

No one knew what it was like to be shocked by an electric eel until 2017, when a professor volunteered to find out—by putting his arm right in the tank! The eel jumped out of the water and into the air, clinging to the researcher's arm to deliver volleys of electricity. The scientist couldn't help but jerk his arm away from the pain, but after 10 tries, he was finally able to get a reading: The pulses were nearly 10 times the strength of a stun gun!

HIGH-FLYING DREAMS

SECRETS ≫≫≫ of a MONGOLIAN

A 13-year-old girl stands tall atop a rocky outcrop in the mountains of western Mongolia. She raises her leather-clad fist toward the sky. On her hand sits a huge golden eagle, her massive wings raised. The girl launches the eagle skyward, and the huge bird takes off, soaring to hunt for prey in the landscape below.

The girl is Aisholpan Nurgaiv. For centuries, both the men and women of her people, the Kazakhs, used to hunt with eagles. But today, most eagle hunters are male. Aisholpan is shaking things up. With her golden eagle at her side, she is bringing back a tradition of her people that stretches back centuries to ancient female huntresses who sent their golden eagles into the skies of the Central Asian steppes centuries ago.

Bird Buddy

The Kazakh people, who live in one mountain range in western Mongolia, are among the only humans on Earth who hunt with golden eagles today. When Aisholpan started out, there were about 400 hunters—all men. Even though she knew she would be the only girl, she wanted to try hunting anyway. But before she could do that, she had to find a wild eagle to call her own.

Female golden eagles are preferred for hunting, because they are much larger and fiercer than the males—an adult female golden eagle can weigh up to 16 pounds (7 kg), and have a 7.5-foot (2.3-m) wingspan! The eagle parents protect their babies ferociously. But that didn't stop Aisholpan. As her ancestors have done for hundreds of years, the young girl climbed down a sheer cliff to the nest, a rope around her waist her only safeguard against a fall. The angry eagles circled overhead. But nothing could discourage Aisholpan, and she successfully captured the eaglet that would become her partner.

Aisholpan slowly taught the wild creature to trust her and depend on her for food. That's how Kazakh hunters train golden eagles, says Adrienne Mayor, a historian at Stanford University in California, U.S.A. "They don't tame the eagle. It's basically a wild animal that they become partners with," she says. After about seven to ten years, Aisholpan will follow Kazakh

People have been hunting with birds of prey for 4,000 years.

EAGLE HUNTRESS

tradition and let her eagle go free. The eagle will return to the wild and raise its own family—a new generation of golden eagles that will help the Kazakhs hunt.

Historic Huntresses

Aisholpan is part of a history that stretches back centuries. "The steppe people live in this very barren and harsh land," says Mayor. "But they created this culture always on the move, and if you have a horse, a dog, and an eagle, you've got it made."

The Kazakh people are nomads who constantly travel. Since they depend on horses to carry them across the desolate landscape, every member of the group has always learned to ride at a young age, explains Mayor. "Kids start

when they're as young as two years old," she says. "They can ride bareback with no reins or saddle." Both boys and girls learn to shoot with a bow and arrow before they reach age five. They train dogs and eagles to help them. Every member of the group learns these skills because all must help hunt. "And traditionally whoever was the best hunter got to lead the hunting band— no matter whether that person was a man or a woman," says Mayor.

Archaeologists have unearthed evidence of some of these ancient female eagle huntresses. A mummified woman buried with a leather eagle-hunting mitt dates back to the fourth or third century B.C., and a gold ring that shows a woman hunting with her eagle dates from 425 B.C.—nearly 2,500

years ago! But as time passed, fewer and fewer women donned the leather glove of the eagle hunter.

New Traditions

Aisholpan trained hard, working with her eagle even through the extreme Mongolian winter, when temperatures fall to minus 58°F (-50°C). Her dedication paid off. In 2014, she became the first woman ever to enter—and win— Mongolia's annual Golden Eagle Festival.

Even though she's proven she can compete as well as the men—and the huntresses who came thousands of years before her—Aisholpan has other big dreams: She plans to attend medical school and become a doctor.

Braving swarms of **angry BEES** honey hunters in Nepal climb 300 feet (91 m) up sheer cliffs.

IS THE FEAT WORTH THE TREAT?

The Himalayan mountains of central Nepal are home to *Apis dorsata laboriosa*, the largest honeybee in the world. Its honey is prized as a tea ingredient in Japan, China, and Korea and can sell for up to $80 a pound! But collecting the sweet nectar is a risky business. The local people scale the sheer cliffs where the bees make their nests, climbing as high as a 30-story building with only homemade rope ladders to hold them!

While scaling their shaky rope ladders and waving away angry bees, they carry two 24-foot (7-m)-long bamboo poles, one to pry the nests off the rock, and the other to hold a basket against the cliff face to catch the falling honeycombs. When they're done collecting, they hoist their 44 pounds (20 kg) of honey for the long trek home.

SECRETS OF
SPACE

Get ready to blast off past the limits of what you can believe! Some of the universe's biggest mysteries are hidden in the stars and planets beyond Earth. This chapter reveals secrets about black holes, life as an astronaut, and planets made of steam, lava—and even diamond! They might seem made up, but they're 100 percent real. After you finish reading this chapter about super stellar space, you'll know one thing for sure: The truth is much, much stranger than science fiction.

The star system is named after a pair of telescopes in Belgium that discovered it.

ARE WE ALONE?

SECRETS of ANOTHER

H ave you ever looked up at the stars and wondered if there's anyone—or anything—out there looking back at you? For decades, scientists have been searching the skies for planets that might be good homes for other life-forms. And now, they might have found some right in our own galactic neighborhood.

On February 22, 2017, NASA announced the discovery of a new solar system just 235 trillion miles (378 trillion km) away. There, seven Earth-size planets orbit a small, red star. Scientists think some could be good homes for life.

A Place to Call Home
The new solar system, called TRAPPIST-1, has seven planets. They're all about the same size as Earth, and scientists think that they all have rocky surfaces, just like our home.

"This is the only star system that we know of so far in the whole universe that has seven Earth-like planets," says astronomer Susan Lederer, part of the team that discovered them. "That makes it really exciting!"

Scientists think that all life-forms must have liquid water to survive. That means their planet has to be exactly the right distance from its star. "If you're too close, it will be too hot and the water will burn away. If you're

too far, it will be too cold and the water will freeze solid. But if you're right in the middle, it will be just right," says Lederer. "So we call this area the Goldilocks Zone." She and her team think that at least three of the TRAPPIST-1 planets are in the Goldilocks Zone.

Who Goes There?
If alien creatures do crawl across the planets' rocky surfaces, what might they look like? "They could be something as simple as bacteria," says Lederer. On Earth, bacteria can live anywhere: in superheated lakes, at the bottom of the ocean, and on every inch of your skin.

The planets are so close together that if you were standing on one, the others would look twice as big as our moon in the sky.

Scientists think the newly discovered solar system could be home to alien life.

If you lived on TRAPPIST 1-b, you'd have a birthday every day and a half. That's how long a year lasts there.

SOLAR SYSTEM

If the planets are home to bigger creatures, they would probably look nothing like humans. Unlike our sun, the TRAPPIST-1 star gives off dim red light. So any plants that grow there might have red leaves, which would be better at absorbing that light, Lederer says. "Their trees might have fall colors all year-round."

And if the TRAPPIST-1 planets have animals, they probably wouldn't see like we do. They might have infrared vision that would help them find their way by their star's light. Infrared is a kind of light humans can't see: We can only feel it as heat.

What's Next

Not all experts are convinced the new planets would be nice places to live. Earth rotates as it orbits around the sun: That's what gives us our day and night. But the TRAPPIST-1 sun's gravity may pull on its planets so hard that they can't rotate. They would have one burning hot side where it is always day. The other side would be a freezing cold place where night never ends.

"I don't think these planets are like Earth at all," says astrophysicist Laurance Doyle. He thinks that the planets still could have liquid water. But only if some of them have an atmosphere (the layer of gases that surround a planet) that is very different from Earth's, with a lot of carbon dioxide and hydrogen.

The TRAPPIST-1 team hopes to find out what the planets' atmospheres are made of soon. In 2018, NASA is planning to launch a powerful telescope called the James Webb Space Telescope. It will be able to see what gases make up the planets' atmospheres.

Scientists are especially excited to look for certain types of oxygen called O_2 and O_3. Experts think these gases can only be created by living things. So far, Earth is the only known planet that has them. Lederer says if the James Webb telescope sees them, "The only explanation will be that we have found life on another planet."

STRANGE SPACE

FORGET ABOUT ALIEN SPACESHIPS. THERE'S ENOUGH REAL-LIFE WEIRD STUFF IN SPACE TO KEEP YOU WONDERING AS YOU STARE INTO THE NIGHT SKY. From ice volcanoes to crushing gravity to colorful clouds that look like Earth objects, outer space is brimming with sights so bizarre, they're hard to believe.

BLACK HOLES

Created when a massive star dies and collapses in on itself, black holes have such intense gravity that anything that gets too close gets pulled inside. Nothing can move fast enough to escape the pull of a black hole's gravity—not even light, the fastest thing in the universe. If you were to fall into one, you would experience a phenomenon called spaghettification, in which your body would be stretched into a long, thin noodle shape. Ouch!

ICE VOLCANOES

Earth isn't the only planet with volcanoes. Saturn's moon Enceladus has them, too. But instead of spraying molten rock, these volcanoes spew something else—ice! Experts think that Saturn's powerful gravity disrupts the interior of Enceladus, where there is a giant underground ocean. When this water comes to the surface and hits the vacuum of space, it instantly freezes. These ice volcanoes blast at 800 miles an hour (1,287 km/h).

SPACE UNICORN

Nebulae are gigantic clouds of gas and dust that can be trillions of miles across. They are the nurseries of the universe, where stars are first born. When viewed through special telescopes, they look like colorful, fluffy clouds. And just like clouds, nebulae can sometimes take shapes familiar to the human eye. There's one that looks like a waterfall, another that looks like a necklace, and even one that looks like a fried egg! But the oddest one of all is the Trifid Nebula, part of which looks a bit like a colorful unicorn!

LONELY PLANETS

Most planets, like the eight that make up our solar system, travel around a star in orderly orbits. But not rogue planets. These intergalactic rebels don't belong to any solar system. They were thrown away from their stars during the formations of their solar systems, and now they float through the universe without a place to call home. Because they don't have suns to heat them up, rogue planets have frozen surfaces. Astronomers estimate there could be billions of them traveling through outer space.

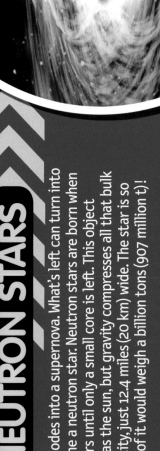

MIGHTY NEUTRON STARS

When a giant star dies, it explodes into a supernova. What's left can turn into a black hole—or it can become a neutron star. Neutron stars are born when a star blows off its outer layers until only a small core is left. This object is about 1.4 times as massive as the sun, but gravity compresses all that bulk into something the size of a city, just 12.4 miles (20 km) wide. The star is so dense that a single teaspoon of it would weigh a billion tons (907 million t)!

Life on
MARS

Get ready to blast off!

NASA hopes to send astronauts to Mars by the 2030s, when today's kids will be adults. That means you might be one of the first to strap in for the 140-million-mile (225-million-km) journey! Read on to find out what the red planet might be like when you land.

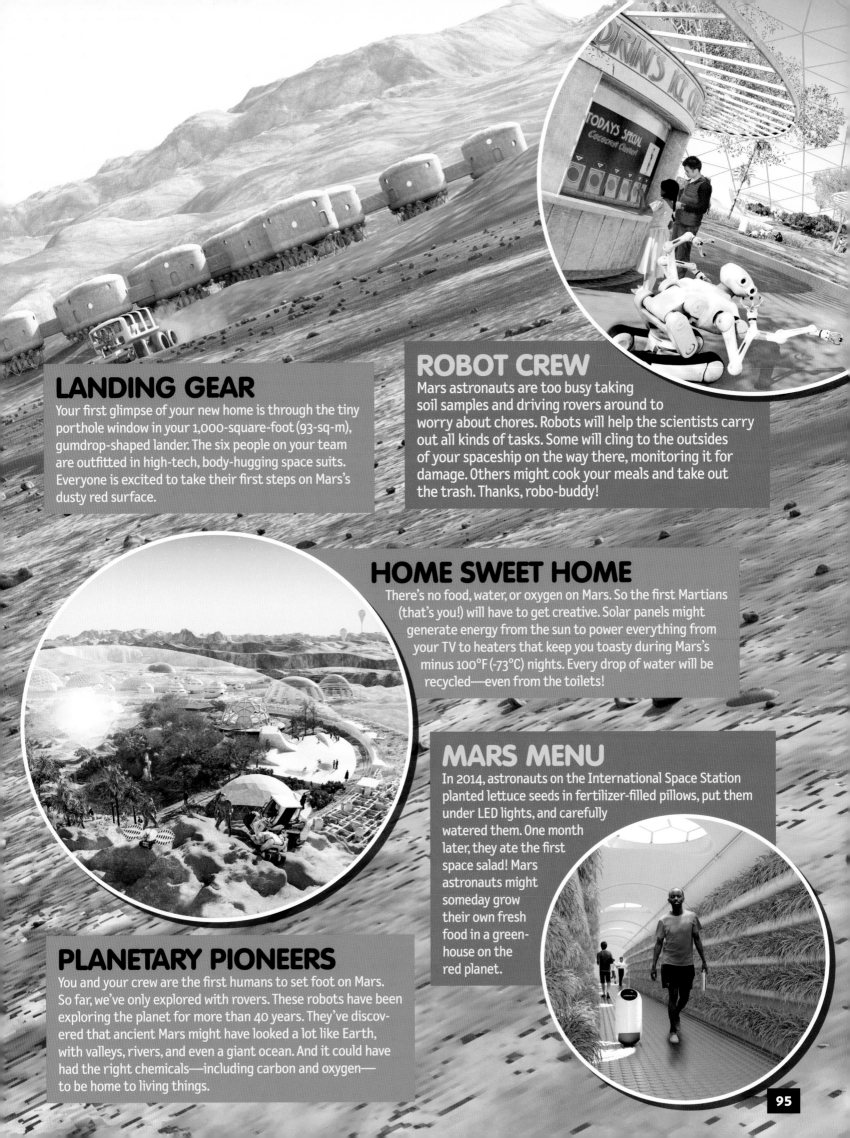

LANDING GEAR

Your first glimpse of your new home is through the tiny porthole window in your 1,000-square-foot (93-sq-m), gumdrop-shaped lander. The six people on your team are outfitted in high-tech, body-hugging space suits. Everyone is excited to take their first steps on Mars's dusty red surface.

ROBOT CREW

Mars astronauts are too busy taking soil samples and driving rovers around to worry about chores. Robots will help the scientists carry out all kinds of tasks. Some will cling to the outsides of your spaceship on the way there, monitoring it for damage. Others might cook your meals and take out the trash. Thanks, robo-buddy!

HOME SWEET HOME

There's no food, water, or oxygen on Mars. So the first Martians (that's you!) will have to get creative. Solar panels might generate energy from the sun to power everything from your TV to heaters that keep you toasty during Mars's minus 100°F (-73°C) nights. Every drop of water will be recycled—even from the toilets!

MARS MENU

In 2014, astronauts on the International Space Station planted lettuce seeds in fertilizer-filled pillows, put them under LED lights, and carefully watered them. One month later, they ate the first space salad! Mars astronauts might someday grow their own fresh food in a green-house on the red planet.

PLANETARY PIONEERS

You and your crew are the first humans to set foot on Mars. So far, we've only explored with rovers. These robots have been exploring the planet for more than 40 years. They've discovered that ancient Mars might have looked a lot like Earth, with valleys, rivers, and even a giant ocean. And it could have had the right chemicals—including carbon and oxygen— to be home to living things.

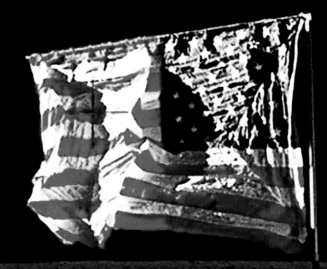

Astronauts' FOOTPRINTS

on the **moon** will last up to 100 million years.

THESE FAMOUS FOOTPRINTS REFUSE TO BE FORGOTTEN!

It's been decades since astronauts first stepped on the moon. But their footprints are still there—and they aren't disappearing anytime soon. That's because unlike Earth, the moon has no atmosphere, so there's no wind to wipe away the prints. And all the moon's water is frozen in ice, so there's no water to wash them away, either. But the prints won't last forever. The lunar surface is constantly bombarded with tiny space rocks called meteorites. Eventually, these impacts will wear away the space boot imprints. But it's a slow process: Scientists estimate it might take between 10 and 100 million years. One small step for man; one long-lasting landmark for mankind.

REACHING THE STARS

The universe is big. Really big. The closest star system to Earth is called Alpha Centauri. At 4.3 light-years away, it's practically our next-door neighbor compared to the other stars in the sky. But it's still about 25 trillion miles (40 trillion km) away. It would take the spacecraft that carried humans to the moon about 165,000 years to reach Alpha Centauri.

Cosmologist Stephen Hawking thought that was too long. The famous thinker backed a far-out idea that could shorten the trip to Alpha Centauri to just 20 years.

BIG BREAKTHROUGH

The project is called Breakthrough Starshot. The idea is to put a space probe on a tiny computer chip, about the size of a postage stamp. This Star-Chip will be attached to a superthin sail made of reflective material. The StarChip and its sail will be launched from a mother ship. Once the tiny craft is in orbit, a laser beam from Earth will be aimed at the sail.

The StarChip would be about the size of a postage stamp, and the sail pulling it would be about three feet (1 m) across.

When light hits an object, it has a pushing force. (This is the reason a comet's tail points away from the sun; the sun's light is forcing it back.) The laser's light will bounce off the StarChip's sail, pushing the craft forward. The Breakthrough Starshot team calculates that after about two minutes, the StarChip will reach about 20 percent of the speed of light. That's 1,000 times faster than the fastest spacecraft today.

LIGHT SPEED

On Earth, the air around us creates friction that slows down our cars and planes. But in space, there's very little friction. Once the sailing spacecraft reaches its top speed, it could coast all the way to its destination. The StarChip could reach Pluto in just three days, and get to Alpha Centauri in about 20 years. The team hopes to launch a fleet of StarChips toward Alpha Centauri. Once they arrived at their intergalactic destination, the tiny crafts will take photos and send scientific information back to Earth—which will take about four years.

The team says that all the technology needed to make Breakthrough Starshot happen has already been invented, or is coming soon. If they can pull off the project, it might be just a few decades until humans reach the stars—at least the one closest to home—for the very first time.

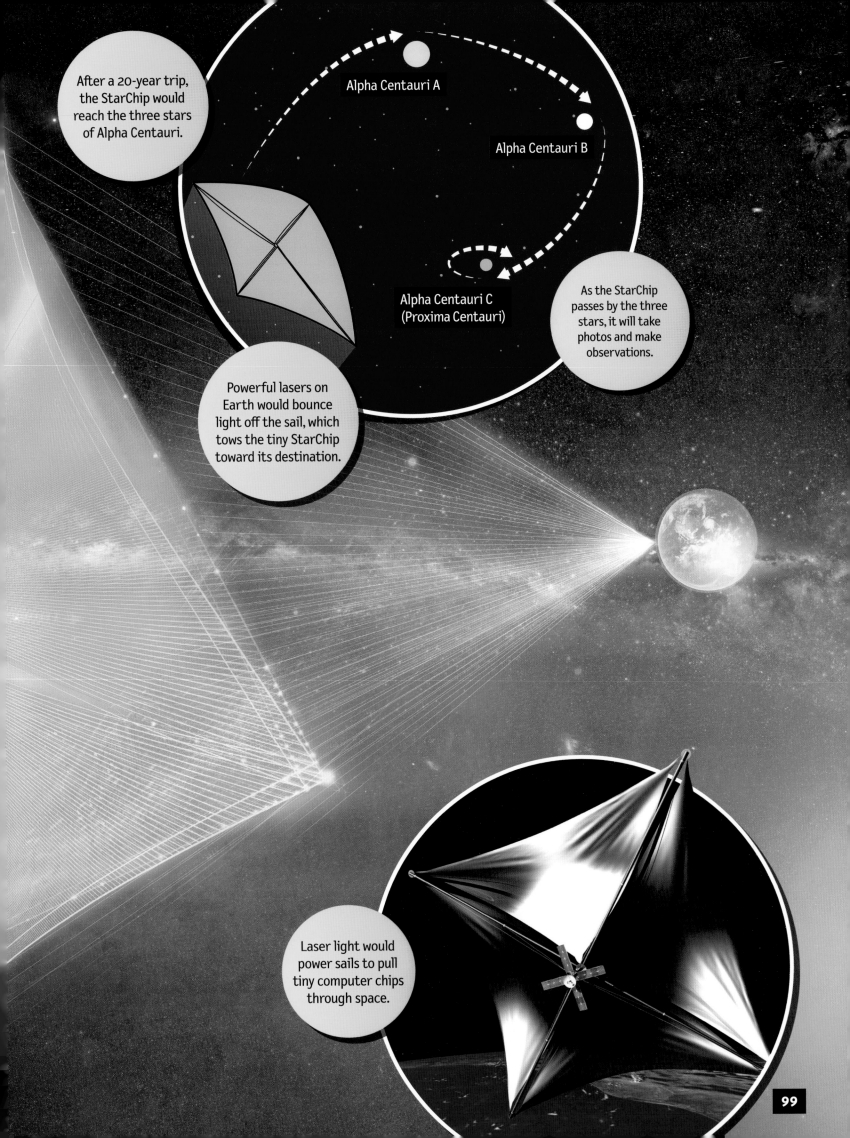

After a 20-year trip, the StarChip would reach the three stars of Alpha Centauri.

Alpha Centauri A

Alpha Centauri B

Alpha Centauri C (Proxima Centauri)

As the StarChip passes by the three stars, it will take photos and make observations.

Powerful lasers on Earth would bounce light off the sail, which tows the tiny StarChip toward its destination.

Laser light would power sails to pull tiny computer chips through space.

It's a weird-but-true side effect of space travel: Astronauts can measure up to two full inches (5.1 cm) taller while zipping around outside Earth's atmosphere than they were on the ground.

Why are astronauts taller in space?

THE EXPERT: Dr. Steve Hart, a NASA aerospace medical doctor who keeps astronauts healthy

Astronauts' faces become puffy when they are in space because weightlessness shifts their body fluids around.

Q WHAT HAPPENS IN YOUR BODY WHEN YOU'RE IN SPACE?

A: Changes start to happen as soon as you enter zero gravity. When you or I are standing on the ground here on Earth, gravity is pulling blood and other body fluids down toward our feet and legs. That's what your body is used to. When you go into space, all that fluid rises up into your chest and head.

Astronauts will get headaches and stuffy noses from the extra fluid in their heads. When they come back, all the fluid suddenly drops back into their legs—sometimes that even makes them pass out!

When astronauts land back on Earth, they have trouble adjusting. Many report forgetting that objects will fall instead of float when they let go of them!

Q YIKES! HOW CAN SPACE TRAVEL MAKE YOU GROW TALLER?

A: Your spine is made up of bones called vertebrae. In between your vertebrae, you have discs filled with a jellylike substance. When you're walking around on Earth, gravity is constantly squeezing those discs, squashing your spine and making it shorter. Even on Earth, people are actually slightly taller in the morning when they get out of bed than they are at the end of the day!

In the zero gravity of space, there's no weight squeezing those discs. They expand. That's what makes astronauts taller in space. But the effect disappears as soon as they come back down.

Q WHAT ELSE DOES SPACE TRAVEL DO TO THE BODY?

A: On Earth, you're constantly working your bones and muscles just to stand up against the force of gravity. But if you don't use it, you lose it! In space, the bones and muscles get smaller and weaker because they lose minerals and calcium. You can lose 20 percent of your muscle mass up there if you're not careful. Astronauts exercise about 2.5 hours a day to slow down this loss.

One kind of gross effect is that after about three months in space, the bottoms of astronauts' feet peel off. You may not think about it, but you have a big callus on the bottom of your feet from walking around. Astronauts get calluses on the tops of their feet, because they hook their feet on stuff to anchor themselves so they don't float away when they're working.

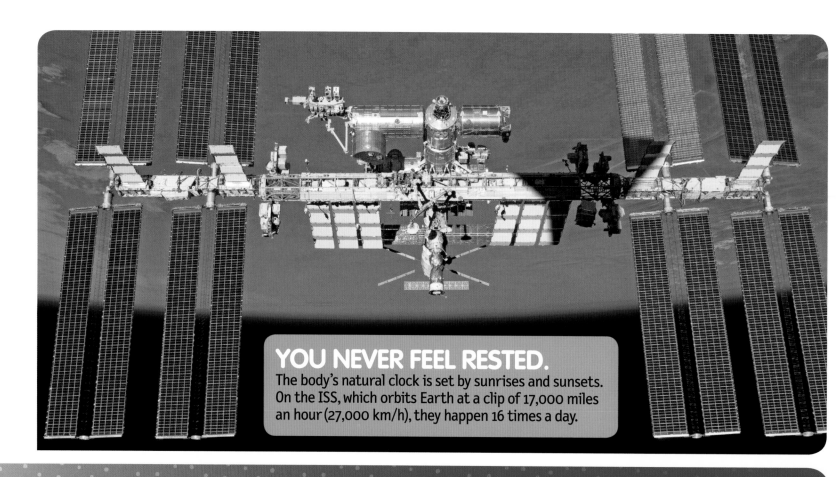

YOU NEVER FEEL RESTED.

The body's natural clock is set by sunrises and sunsets. On the ISS, which orbits Earth at a clip of 17,000 miles an hour (27,000 km/h), they happen 16 times a day.

SECRETS ABOUT LIFE IN SPACE

TWO HUNDRED AND FIFTY MILES (402 KM) ABOVE THE EARTH FLOATS A GIANT METAL STRUCTURE WITH WINGS MADE OF SOLAR PANELS. IT LOOKS LIKE SOMETHING STRAIGHT OUT OF SCIENCE FICTION. IT'S THE INTERNATIONAL SPACE STATION (ISS), AND IT'S BEEN HOME TO ASTRONAUTS SINCE 2000. WORKING ON THIS SKY-HIGH SCIENCE LAB IS ONE OF THE COOLEST JOBS THERE IS. BUT BEING AN ASTRO-NAUT ISN'T ALWAYS GLAMOROUS.

SPACE HAS A FUNNY SMELL.

It's kind of like charcoal and burning plastic, and it comes from dying stars. Tiny particles cling to astronauts' suits during space walks, and they carry them back inside the ISS.

YOU'RE GOING TO GET SPACESICK.

Almost every astronaut does. The sudden loss of gravity changes the brain, which mysteriously responds by making the body vomit. Despite decades of research, scientists haven't figured out a cure.

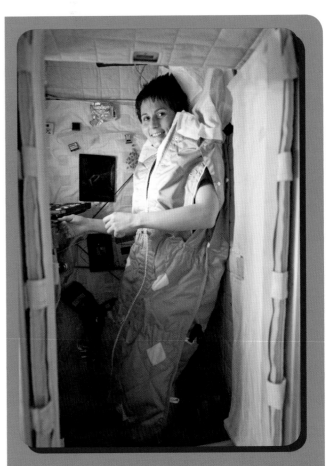

YOU DON'T SHOWER.

It would be impossible in zero gravity, so sponge baths are all you get. Most astronauts are assigned to the ISS for about six months. But the record for the longest spaceflight goes to Russian cosmonaut Valeri Polyakov, who spent 438 days on the Mir space station. *Pee-yew!*

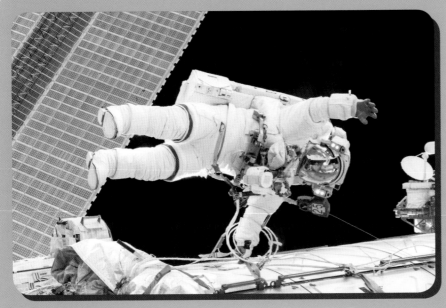

YOU HAVE TO WEAR DIAPERS UNDER YOUR SPACE SUIT.

When you gotta go, you gotta go. Space walks can last hours, and there aren't a lot of rest stops floating around in the cosmos.

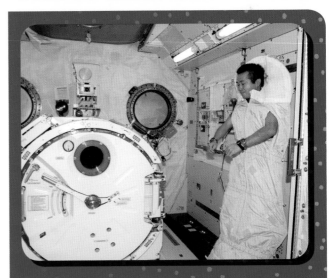

FOOD TASTES AWFUL.

It's all freeze-dried mush, but that's not the only problem. Without gravity to pull body fluids down, astronauts' sinuses get clogged, dulling their sense of taste. To compensate, they go through a lot of hot sauce!

YOU HAVE TO SLEEP NEXT TO A FAN.

If you don't, you'll die. That's because the carbon dioxide you breathe out doesn't blow away from your body in zero gravity. Instead, it forms a bubble around you, blocking your oxygen intake.

SECRETS of a HIDDEN

Way out in the farthest reaches of the solar system, a mysterious undiscovered planet orbits through space. It's gigantic—almost four times the size of Earth. And it's so far away that it takes up to 20,000 years to go around the sun.

This planet isn't science fiction. Astronomers think it really exists. They've dubbed it Planet Nine, and they're searching the skies to find it.

Far Out

When most people think of our solar system, they think of its eight planets and our sun. But not astronomer Mike Brown. Brown is interested in the region of space beyond these eight planets. "There's this huge part of the solar system that we're only just beginning to learn about," he says.

Beyond Neptune is an area known as the Kuiper (KY-per) belt, which scientists used to think was empty. But it turns out the Kuiper belt is actually home to icy, rocky objects; billions of comets; and a few dwarf planets (objects too small to be considered planets) such as Pluto.

While observing the belt in 2014, Brown and his research partner, Konstantin Batygin, saw something strange: The orbits of many of the smaller objects in the Kuiper belt were aligned. Weirder still, they never came closer to the sun than Neptune. It was like something was pulling them away. But what?

Strange Space

Brown and Batygin spent over a year trying to figure out the objects' odd behavior. They discussed several potential answers—but only one seemed to

Some scientists think Planet Nine could have once been a free-floating world that was snagged by our sun's gravity.

In April 2017, citizen scientists searched the skies and found four objects that could be Planet Nine!

WORLD

work. "We were convinced another planet was out there," Brown says.

To find out if they were right, the pair created a computer model illustrating the objects. Then they plugged an imaginary planet into the model. The model showed that the planet's gravity would pull on these icy objects, making them move in exactly the way they had moved in space. The model also gave the scientists an idea of the planet's size. Because of its strong gravitational pull, Brown and Batygin inferred that the planet would be roughly the size of Neptune. Like Neptune, it would likely be made of gas, and the temperature there would be a frigid minus 375°F (-226°C).

"It's hard to believe that we could miss something as big as Neptune," Brown says. But it is *really* far away, about 56 billion miles (90 billion km) from Earth. Only a very small amount of the sun's light would hit it. If Planet Nine exists, only two telescopes in the world are powerful enough to search vast areas of the sky for it efficiently—and until now, they haven't been looking for it.

The Search Is On
Brown and Batygin are convinced that their evidence proves that Planet Nine is hidden somewhere beyond the Kuiper belt. But Brown predicts the search will take at least a few years.

Soon future telescopes will let us peer even farther into space. And when we do, Brown thinks we may discover that Planet Nine isn't the only thing out there. "Planet Nine is the planet for my generation," he says. "But Planet 10? That's what tomorrow's astronomers—kids growing up today—will look for."

EXTREME PLANETS

SOMEWHERE OUT THERE IN THE VASTNESS OF OUR UNIVERSE MIGHT BE A PLANET THAT COULD BE GREAT TO VISIT ONE DAY. These planets, however, wouldn't... unless your idea of a relaxing vacation includes massive storms, crushing gravity, or molten lava. Read on to get a glimpse of these otherworldly wonders.

PINK PLANET

Like Jupiter, planet GJ 504b is made of gas. Unlike Jupiter, it's bright pink! At 460°F (237°C), this planet is the temperature of a hot oven, and its heat makes it glow. At its hot core, the planet is almost red, but when the light hits its clouds, it turns deep magenta.

LAVA PLANET

Like Earth, CoRoT-7b is made mostly of rock. But that's where the similarities end. Superheated temperatures melt the rock into a lava ocean that covers half the planet. The rock ocean vaporizes, turning into rock clouds that condense and—you guessed it—rain down rocks. Watch out below!

STORMY PLANET

Talk about extreme weather! As planet HD 80606b approaches its sun, things get hot—really hot. The temperature climbs to a scorching 2240°F (1227°C), creating a huge buildup of energy that explodes into an enormous storm the width of three Earths. Twin hurricanes spin out of the storm and rip across the planet, leaving behind rivers of glowing gas.

DIAMOND PLANET

Four thousand light-years away, a giant diamond five times the size of planet Earth hangs in the sky. It's a planet made entirely of priceless gem! Long ago, planet PSR J1719-1438b used to be a star. But it got caught in the gravity of a nearby pulsar—a type of collapsed star that shoots out deadly cosmic rays and radiation. Over millions of years, the pulsar's rays carved away the star until just the diamond core was left.

STEAMY PLANET

Dive beneath the billowing clouds on this steamy planet and you'll find a strange sea. At 450°F (232°C), it's so hot on planet GJ 1214b that all water is instantly turned into steam. At the planet's core, the heat and pressure are so intense that they squeeze water molecules together until they become a fluid-like substance called plasma. The plasma sea glows with neon orange light.

BRAIN-BOGGLING
BODY

You might think you know yourself pretty well, but your own body holds all kinds of secrets. Did you know that your brain is powered by electricity? Or that your awesome anatomy is home to a rain forest of tiny microbes that crawl through your eyelashes and swing from your hair? New research has helped scientists unravel many of the mysteries of us. Read on to learn about some of their most exciting discoveries.

Most people have about **67** different kinds of **BACTERIA** living in their **BELLY BUTTONS.**

IT'S A JUNGLE IN THERE!

Have you ever wondered what's inside your belly button? You might think there's probably some dirt, and maybe even some lint. But that's not all. A group of researchers from North Carolina, U.S.A., decided to find out. They swabbed the belly buttons of 60 brave volunteers to see what was lurking inside.

What the team found shocked them: 2,368 species of bacteria were growing in those 60 belly buttons. And the researchers think 1,458 of them may be totally new to science! The volunteers had an average of 67 kinds of bacteria living in their belly buttons. One volunteer had a type of bacteria that had only ever been found in Japan—where he had never been. Another hosted microbes that usually only live in ice caps and thermal vents. And most of the species found in one belly button weren't in the others. That shows there is almost certainly no one else on Earth with your exact collection of microbes.

Some belly buttons are home to a type of yellow slime mold that is usually found in rotting logs.

Scientists swabbed belly buttons, then grew the bacteria inside to reveal the unique set of microbes each person was carrying around.

HEAT DETECTOR

What if you didn't need any light at all to see? Snakes called pit vipers are named for the small divots on their face between their nostrils and eyes. These pits detect infrared radiation, a type of light humans can't see, but can feel as heat. The pit viper's special sensors give the snake a heat map of its environment, allowing it to "see" warm prey even in pitch-blackness.

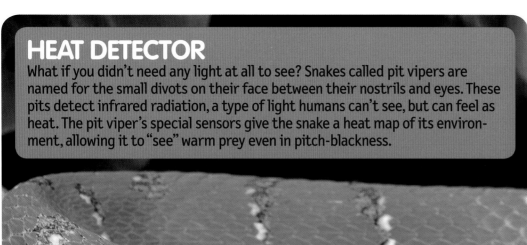

AWESOME ANIMAL ANATOMY

BUILT-IN FLASHLIGHT

Wouldn't it be nice to click on your built-in headlamp every time you need to get up for a glass of water at night? The smalltooth dragonfish has not just one, but three flashlights: a blue one, a red one, and an orange one. Most sea creatures can see blue light, but not red light. So when the dragonfish gets hungry, it switches on its red flashlight to hunt, with its prey none the wiser. Its orange light is still a mystery to science.

YOUR BODY IS TRULY INCREDIBLE. IT CAN SMACK A BASEBALL ACROSS A FIELD, SEE ALL THE COLORS OF THE RAINBOW, AND NEVER MISS A MOVE WHEN GREETING YOUR FRIENDS WITH YOUR SUPER-SECRET HANDSHAKE. BUT READ ON ABOUT THE SPECIAL BODY PARTS ONLY SOME ANIMALS HAVE, AND YOU MIGHT START TO FEEL A LITTLE JEALOUS.

EXTRA LEG

Everyone knows kangaroos can really hop to it. But these Australian animals actually spend most of their time walking on all fours—actually, on all *fives*. In 2014, scientists discovered that kangaroos also use their tail for getting around. The researchers videotaped kangaroos as they crawled across a platform. With each stride, the animals pushed off with their tail to give themselves an extra boost.

NATURAL GOGGLES

Imagine speeding down the highway with no windshield. It sounds exhilarating ... until you think about the bugs and dust the wind would fling into your eyes. Yuck! Birds face the same problem, but they've developed a clever solution: a set of third eyelids that they can close to protect their eyes from debris when they zip across the sky. Many animals, from polar bears to camels, also have these built-in goggles.

SNOUT SENSOR

With its beaver tail, duck-like bill, and venomous stingers on its hind feet, the platypus is one odd animal. The first scientists to see one thought someone was playing a joke on them! But the platypus is even stranger than it seems: Its snout is covered with sensors that detect electrical charges. That helps the animal track down potential meals hiding in dark water.

THIRD EYE

Two eyes are enough ... or are they? Some lizards have a patch of light-sensitive cells on their head called the parietal eye. To figure out what this extra eye does, scientists taught a group of lizards to swim from the center of a small swimming pool to a hidden ledge at its edge. Then the scientists covered the lizards' parietal eyes with a special paint and had the lizards try again. The creatures swam in circles, unable to locate the ledge. Researchers think the third eye likely uses sunlight to judge direction. Humans actually have a parietal eye, too, but ours isn't so useful—it's hidden underneath our skulls.

YUCKY You

You might shower every day and never forget to floss.

But even the cleanest human is still a stinky, snotty, sweaty creature. If you still think the ick doesn't apply to you, read on for some shockingly gross secrets going on right underneath your nose (and sometimes even inside it!).

CREEPY CRAWLY

On every square inch (6.5 sq cm) of your skin, there are as many as 32 million bacteria wiggling away. Different spots are home to different sorts of microbes: The ones that live inside your nose are totally different from the ones between your toes.

FACE FEAST

Think you're squeaky clean? Think again. Tiny mites, so small a dozen of them could fit on the head of a pin, spend their lives on your face, munching on your dead skin cells and oils.

WINDY CONDITIONS

The average person passes gas between 10 and 23 times a day. Some people can produce two liters of gas a day—that's enough gas to fill a large soda bottle! Certain foods, like beans and broccoli, can make the stomach create extra gas.

TUMMY TRICK

Your stomach uses acid to break down your dinner so it can be digested. Called hydrochloric acid, it's strong enough to dissolve metal.

SUPER SOAKER

The typical adult sweats enough each year to fill 60 gallon milk jugs (227 L). Humans have between two and four million sweat glands on their bodies. They are most numerous on the palms of the hands and soles of the feet.

DUST OFF

You shed about eight pounds (3.6 kg) of skin cells each year. So the next time you notice the dust that collects on your TV and windows, don't forget—you're looking at dead bits of you!

THIRSTY YET?

You produce about 1.5 quarts (1.42 L) of snot every day—and you swallow almost all of it. That might sound gross, but you wouldn't be alive without it. Your mucus helps keep your airways from drying out, and catches dust and debris so it doesn't enter your lungs.

SPIT SECRET

The average kid produces about one pint (0.5 L) of saliva every day. It would take you a year to fill a bathtub with spit. In 8,345 years, you could fill an Olympic-size swimming pool!

115

CONTORTIONISTS

showcase their

super bendy bodies

by **twisting** themselves into **crazy shapes** and positions.

But contortionists aren't double-jointed—it's a myth.

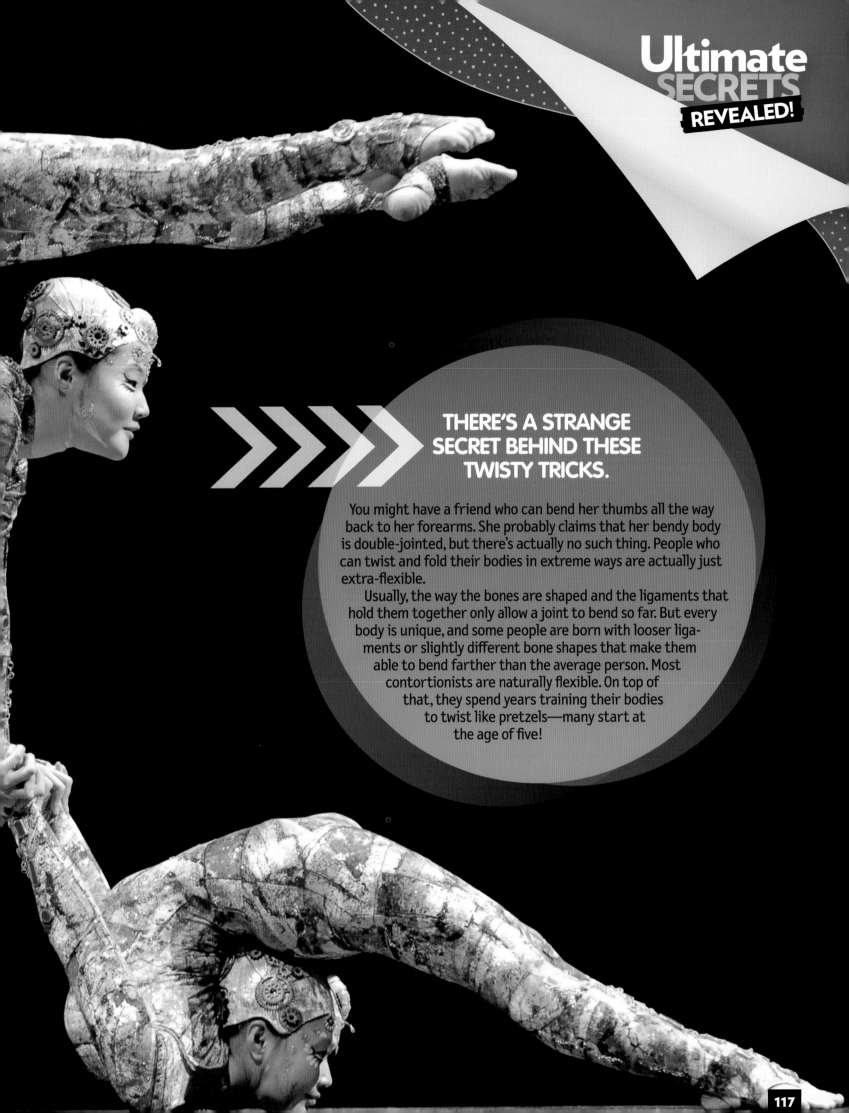

THERE'S A STRANGE SECRET BEHIND THESE TWISTY TRICKS.

You might have a friend who can bend her thumbs all the way back to her forearms. She probably claims that her bendy body is double-jointed, but there's actually no such thing. People who can twist and fold their bodies in extreme ways are actually just extra-flexible.

Usually, the way the bones are shaped and the ligaments that hold them together only allow a joint to bend so far. But every body is unique, and some people are born with looser ligaments or slightly different bone shapes that make them able to bend farther than the average person. Most contortionists are naturally flexible. On top of that, they spend years training their bodies to twist like pretzels—many start at the age of five!

Scientists use brain scanning technology to understand what different areas of the brain do and study the impacts of disease and injuries.

POWERED BY ELECTRICITY

SECRETS of the BRAIN

Without electricity, you wouldn't be reading this right now. And not because the lights would shut off—it's because your *brain* would shut off.

The brain uses more power than any other organ in your body—about 20 percent of the energy you get from the food you eat heads to your noggin. Your brain uses this energy to generate electricity. It makes enough to light up a lightbulb! But how does the same force that toasts your bread power your head?

Charged Up

You're doing your homework at the kitchen table when you see your baby brother out of the corner of your eye. He's reaching up to get his juice off the counter and—*oh no!*—he's about to touch the hot stove! You spring up from your chair, dive toward him, and knock his hand out of the way. *Phew!* But wait ... how exactly did you perform this split-second feat?

Your brain is packed with cells called neurons. Neurons use the power of electricity to carry messages. There are about 86 billion of them in your noggin—that's such a big number it would take you 3,000 years to count them all! These neurons are how your brain communicates with your body. Messages zip from your head to your toes by hopping from neuron to neuron. It's like a mental relay race.

Power Play

When one of your neurons is resting, its insides have a negative electrical charge, and its outsides have a positive charge. When your brain decides to send out a message, it tells the neuron to swap the charges: its outside becomes negative and its inside positive. This generates an electric charge. The charge triggers the next neuron in line to swap charges, then that one triggers the next in line. This chain reaction is how messages travel from one neuron to another.

When you saw your baby brother reaching for the hot stove, your brain sent messages bouncing along your neurons to your body. It told your feet to leap across the room, and your

While you're dreaming, your body paralyzes your muscles so you can't act out your dreams and hurt yourself.

There are as many connections between neurons in your brain as there are stars in 1,500 Milky Way galaxies.

hand to push your brother away from the danger zone. Your heroic action happened so fast thanks to the power of electricity—neurons carry messages at more than 150 miles an hour (241 km/h).

Shocking Secrets

Without electricity, you wouldn't be able to read or understand these words. And it's not just your brain that relies on electricity. Electrical signals also keep your heart pumping in a regular rhythm—that's why medics can sometimes restart a stopped heart with an electrical jolt. An electrical shock like a lightning strike can disrupt the body's electrical system, just like a power surge can fry your computer.

With so much electricity leaping around inside you, it might seem like the human body is a great source of power. Could you use your brain to charge a cell phone? It's possible, but you'd have to be patient: It would take about 70 hours.

Feeling feebleminded? Don't. Your brain's low voltage is actually a big achievement. According to Kwabena Boahen, a computer scientist at Stanford University in California, U.S.A., it would take at least 10 megawatts to operate a robot as smart as a human. That's the same amount of energy produced by a small power plant! Your brain makes you laugh, dance, dream, and crack a joke—all with a tiny fraction of that power.

FIVE MENTAL MYSTERIES

The brain is far more powerful than a supercomputer. So it's no surprise that scientists don't fully understand it yet. Here are five questions they're still trying to answer:

1. **What are emotions?** A video of a shark opening its jaws to strike might make your heart beat faster in fear, while a photo of your family might make you feel love. How does your brain create these emotions?

2. **How does your brain understand time?** Snap your fingers. Because light travels faster than sound, you should have seen the snap before you heard it. But your brain edits the experience to make the sound and sight happen at the same moment. How?

3. **How do we predict the future?** When we make decisions, we think forward to how they'll play out in the future. But how does the brain make these predictions?

4. **How does memory work?** How does the brain decide what to save? Why can we recall some experiences but not others?

5. **Why do we sleep?** We spend about one-third of our lives snoozing. Researchers have found that our brains are highly active while we sleep—but what are they doing?

Smells can bring back memories—even ones you've forgotten!

ORGANIC Sweet Peppers $4/pound

Why do certain smells bring back memories?

THE EXPERT: Rachel Herz is a psychologist at Brown University in Providence, Rhode Island, U.S.A., who specializes in smell and memory.

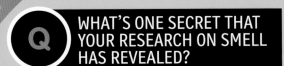

Q: HOW DOES A SMELL TRIGGER A MEMORY?

A: A smell triggers a memory if it's connected to something in our past. If that smell was in the air during a certain event, smelling it again may recall that event.

The sense of smell was the very first sense to evolve. The first living things on Earth were tiny, one-celled creatures. They had to have a way of deciding if something near them was good to eat, or if it was dangerous and they should move away. So they grew a chemical detector in their brains to sense those things. That was the beginning of our sense of smell.

Later, the brain's emotional and memory centers grew out of that part of the brain. That's why those areas are linked today.

Q: HOW ARE SMELL AND MEMORY TIED IN THE BRAIN?

A: When you smell something, that information goes immediately into the amygdala, the part of the brain that processes emotion and memory. Right after that, the information goes to the hippocampus, which is where associations with smell are linked up, and other types of memory are processed.

Information from other senses, such as vision or hearing, can end up in the brain's emotional and memory centers, too. But it has to go through other parts of the brain first. Smells go directly to these centers. That's why when a smell triggers a memory, the memory feels much more vividly emotional. It's also why a smell can transport you to the original time and place.

What that means is that the *emotion* of a memory comes back to you first, before the meaning of the memory. So you might smell something that makes you feel sad, but you won't know why right away. Sometimes, the meaning never comes back to you.

Q: WHAT'S ONE SECRET THAT YOUR RESEARCH ON SMELL HAS REVEALED?

A: This is pretty weird: the name we give a smell can change what it smells like to us. Here's an example: there are two chemicals that, if you mix them together, they can smell like Parmesan cheese—or, they can smell like vomit. I did an experiment where I had people come into the lab, and I told them the smell was Parmesan cheese. Then I asked them questions like, "Do you want to eat it?" They said, "Yes!"

Then a week later, I had them come back to the lab. I gave them the exact same odor to smell, but this time, I told them it was vomit. When I asked them if they wanted to eat it, they were totally grossed out. And they couldn't believe it was the same odor that they had smelled before. But the only thing that changed was the name!

Your hair and fingernails are made of the same thing as a porcupine's QUILLS.

>>>

WHAT DO NAILS AND QUILLS HAVE IN COMMON?

They're made of the same substance—one that also forms horns, feathers, scales, hooves, claws, and many more animal accessories besides. The secret is keratin, a fibrous protein that grows out of the skin. It might be tough to see the similarities between horns and hair. But a rhino's horn is actually made of bundles of hairlike fibers tightly packed together. When exposed to water, keratin softens and swells, making it easy to shape. Ancient humans around the world wore headdresses made of horn, ceremonial clothes made of feathers, and necklaces made of claws. Native Americans used porcupine quills to decorate garments and bags. Even baleen from the mouths of whales, another keratin structure, was once used to make chimney sweep brooms and corsets!

WHAT MAKES US TICKLISH?

Ticklishness is a strange sensation. Why does it make us laugh? Why can't we do it to ourselves? And why does it exist in the first place?

The mystery of ticklishness has left scientists scratching their heads (and probably trying to tickle themselves) for decades. That is until a group of researchers in Berlin, Germany, decided to unravel the mystery ... by tickling rats!

TICKLES IN THE BRAIN

When you tickle your little sister, she probably squeals with delight. Well, rats do this too, by sounding off with high-pitched noises. Scientists think of these sounds as rat giggles. They can't be detected with human ears, so neuroscientist Michael Brecht and his team set up a special device to record them. They set up another device to record the rats' brain activity. Then the researchers performed their serious scientific duty ... they tickled the rats all over!

The scientists noticed that when they tickled a rat, there was a burst of activity in one small part of its brain. "When we activate this section, the animals giggle," says Brecht. "That makes it clear that we probably found the area of the brain that controls ticklishness." In other words, they had found the brain's tickle spot.

Many people are most ticklish on the sides and soles of their feet.

JUMPING FOR JOY

Have you ever noticed that someone's mood can change how ticklish they are? When people are afraid, for example, they aren't very ticklish. The scientists discovered that rats are the same way. When they tried putting the rodents on a high platform under bright lights and then tickling them, the frightened rodents didn't let out a single tee-hee.

The researchers found that, like humans, rats are more ticklish when they're in the right mood. As the scientists tickled them, the rats warmed up to the sensation and giggled more and more. The scientists noticed that sometimes, rats being tickled would even leap into the air in delight! (The German team called these adorable hops *Freudensprünge*, or "joy jumps.") "That made us think they're really having fun!" says Brecht.

PLAY PUZZLE

What about the biggest mystery of ticklishness—why does it exist in the first place? The rat experiment gave the team some ideas. They noticed that when they played with the rats—by training the furry critters to chase their hands around their cages—the rats would chuckle just like they did when they were tickled. If you've ever seen human kids laughing as they chase each other around a playground, you know people do the same thing.

"We think that there is a link in the brain between tickling and play," says Brecht. Maybe, he thinks, whether you're a rat or a human, tickling is a way to have fun together.

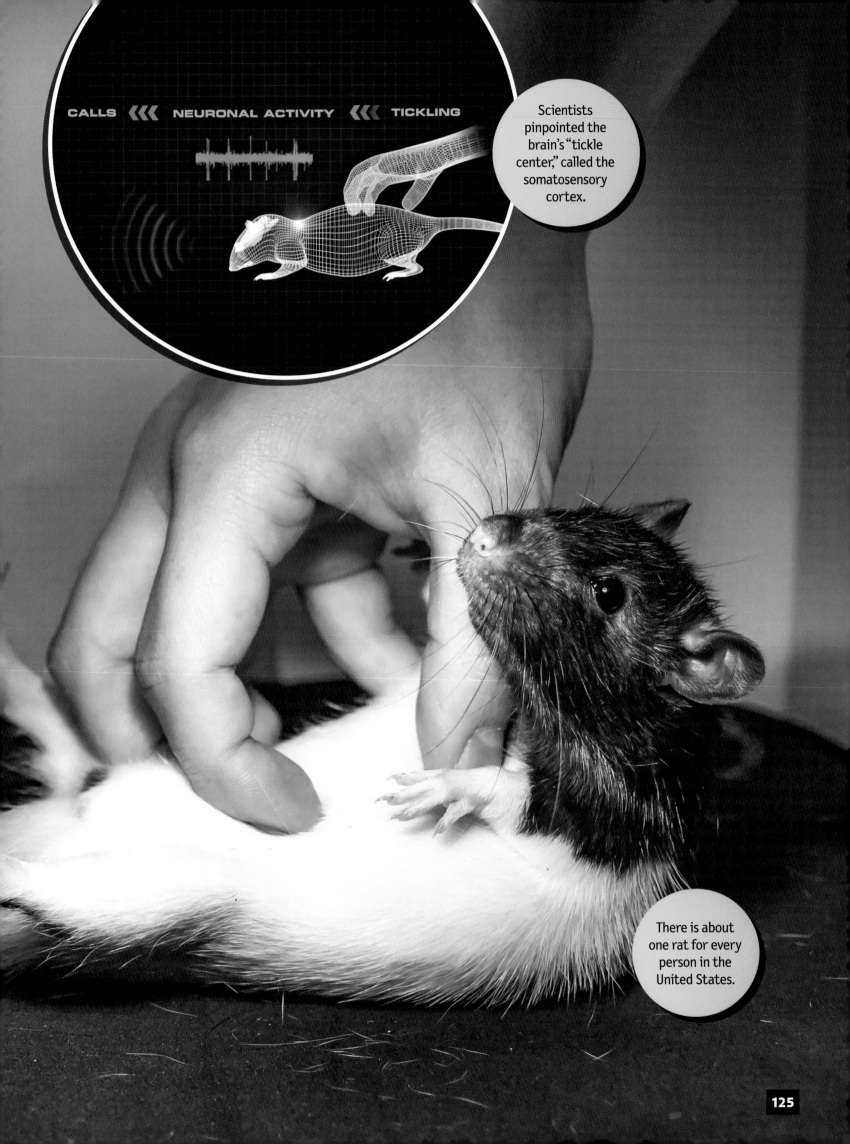

CALLS ≪≪≪ NEURONAL ACTIVITY ≪≪≪ TICKLING

Scientists pinpointed the brain's "tickle center," called the somatosensory cortex.

There is about one rat for every person in the United States.

125

A CLOSER LOOK AT YOU

THESE AREN'T PHOTOS OF FARAWAY STAR SYSTEMS OR SCENES FROM THE DEEP SEA. THEY'RE FROM SOMEWHERE MUCH MORE FAMILIAR—YOU! **Magnified under a microscope, even your closest nooks and crannies look alien.** Take a good look at some of the secrets of you.

FAT CELLS

Our fat cells form a thick layer under our skin that acts like a blanket, cushioning us and keeping us warm. It also stores energy so we can use it when we need it. In this close-up picture, the yellow fat deposits have been removed to show how the cells connect in a structure like a bee's honeycomb.

INFLUENZA VIRUS

Aching muscles, a pounding head, and stuffy nose—the flu is no fun! This H1N1 flu virus caused the 2009 swine flu outbreak. It sent about 61 million people around the world crawling under the covers. Despite its name, the disease wasn't spread by pork products: it happened when several flu viruses joined with one that normally affects pigs, creating a killer combination.

PENICILLIUM FUNGUS

In 1920, a scientist named Alexander Fleming was growing bacteria on plates to study when he made a mistake: He left one of the plates uncovered and went on vacation. When Fleming returned, he noticed that mold had taken over the plate—and somehow, it had stopped the bacteria from growing. He had accidentally discovered the world's first antibiotic: penicillin.

LIVER CELLS

Every time you bite into a sandwich, you should be thanking your liver. That's because this organ changes most of the food you eat into stuff your body can use. While it's at it, the liver cleans your blood, clearing out pollutants, leftover medicines, and other substances you don't want.

BRAIN CELLS

There are more than 86 billion nerve cells, or neurons, in the brain. They use electricity to carry messages that make you think. Neurons get all the attention, but they're not alone up there! There are about the same number of glial cells like these in your noggin. They're the neurons' support system, holding them up and feeding them so they can do their job.

CHAPTER 7

FASCINATING FOOD

Your standard lunchtime sandwich might be tasty, but it's not exactly exciting ... or is it? Be prepared to be amazed. Believe it or not, there are mysteries hiding everywhere—even in your food! Want to be the most interesting person at the table? Read on to learn about pigs that hunt for mushrooms, the science of spice, and a meal that can kill you in minutes. This chapter is jam-packed with an all-you-can-eat buffet of fascinating food secrets!

Some of the world's
BIGGEST
vegetables
are grown in
Alaska, U.S.A.

WHY DO THESE VEGGIES GROW SO GIANT?

At state fairs around the United States, farmers proudly display giant vegetables too big to fit through the door of the average grocery store. But the Alaska State Fair tops them all. Alaska is known for producing some of the world's biggest vegetables. Farmers there have grown broccoli like bushes and cantaloupe like boulders. But in a state known for its cold, why are these vast veggies thriving?

The secret is in Alaska's summer sun, say scientists. Alaska is so far north that during the summer months, the sun sets late and rises early. Crops can get as much as 20 hours of sunlight a day. Since plants harness the energy of the sun to grow, a process called photosynthesis, Alaskan veggies can get much larger than mainland produce. So, if you ever visit the "land of the midnight sun," bring a big appetite!

POISONOUS PUFFERFISH

Travel to Japan, and you'll see it advertised on menus all over. Fugu, or pufferfish, is considered a special treat there. But eater beware: the fish's internal organs contain a toxic substance. A single fish has enough poison to kill 30 people! Chefs train for years to learn how to safely remove the dangerous parts.

MOST DEADLY FOODS

THESE TASTY SNACKS MIGHT LOOK DELICIOUS, BUT THEY ACTUALLY HIDE SCARY SECRETS—THEY'RE SOME OF THE MOST DANGEROUS EATS ON EARTH! YET, DAREDEVIL FOODIES ALL OVER THE WORLD AREN'T AFRAID TO DIG IN. READ ON TO DISCOVER SIX FRIGHTENING FOODS THAT MAY MAKE YOU THINK TWICE BEFORE TUCKING IN.

FREAKY FUNGUS

Never, ever eat a mushroom you find in the wild. Only a few are poisonous enough to kill, but many of the sneaky 'shrooms look exactly like edible varieties. The disguise is so good that even experts can be fooled. One of the deadliest is Europe's death cap mushroom, which kills about half of the people who try a nibble.

TREACHEROUS TENTACLES

In Korea, some daring diners like to slurp up small octopuses. But here's where it gets risky: The sea crawlers are cut up and served while still wiggling! So diners need to be careful. The suction cups on the octopus legs can sometimes stick to the eater's throat on the way down. It's food fighting back!

PUDDING OR POISON?

In the United States, it's known as tapioca, and it's usually found as the star ingredient in pudding. The tasty part comes from the root of the cassava plant, which when raw, contains the deadly poison cyanide. But when properly prepared, it's harmless—and a staple food for 700 million people around the world. So don't worry, your pudding cup is perfectly safe!

FORBIDDEN FRUIT

Unripe ackee fruit contains a poison called hypoglycin that can cause vomiting, coma, or even death. Those brave enough to try ackee anyway must wait until the fruit turns red and the pods open. The taste must be worth the risk—it's the national fruit of Jamaica!

YOU'VE GOT TO BE NUTS

Cashews are a delicious snack. But don't ever eat one from the tree. Most people don't know that even the "raw" cashews sold in stores have been steamed to remove a chemical called urushiol. The itch-causing agent in poison ivy, urushiol can kill if eaten.

Food That FOOLS You

SOAPY ORANGE JUICE

The bubbles in freshly poured juice go flat fast. To keep OJ camera-ready, food stylists mix two drops of soap with some juice, then add the froth to the top of the drink with a spoon.

PIN THE BLUEBERRY ON THE PANCAKE

Stylists don't just toss a handful of berries on top of pancakes and call it a day. They carefully place each plump fruit, using toothpicks to hold them in place so they don't roll away.

SNIP 'N' SPRAY

If pancakes cook up a little lopsided, stylists give them a trim with scissors to make sure they're perfectly round. Sometimes, they spray the stack with a coating normally used to protect furniture. That keeps the syrup from soaking in so it looks perfectly drippy.

FRUIT COLORING

Sliced strawberries often have white insides that aren't so appetizing. So stylists brush red food coloring over the white areas to cover them. Sometimes, they'll use a dab of lipstick instead.

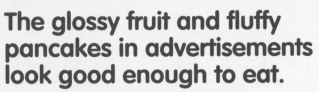

The glossy fruit and fluffy pancakes in advertisements look good enough to eat.

But take a bite and you might be in for a nasty surprise! It's up to food stylists to make sure meals are ready for their close-up—and they've got lots of tricks up their sleeves.

GOT GLUE?

Does this breakfast look suspicious? Cereal usually sinks to the bottom of the bowl. To prop it up to be photographed, stylists put a circular piece of cardboard inside the bowl. Then, instead of milk, they add a thin layer of glue (unlike milk, it doesn't make the flakes soggy) and sprinkle the flakes on top.

SIZZLING SYRUP

Syrup looks better if it's thick. So, before stylists pour it on the flapjack stack, they heat it up to about 270°F (132°C), until the water inside evaporates and the syrup thickens. At that temperature, it would burn your tongue!

TOOLS OF THE TRADE

Lemon juice: Adding it to an apple or banana keeps the fruit from browning.

Glass cleaner: For sopping up greasy spots on plates.

Vegetable oil: Brushing it on vegetables or meat makes them look shiny.

Spray bottle: For adding water droplets that make fruit and veggies look fresh.

SHAPIN' BACON

To make bacon perfectly wavy, stylists first mold a sheet of tinfoil into rows of ridges. Then, they fit the strips of raw bacon over their mold. As the bacon roasts in the oven, it hardens into the shape.

SWEET MYSTERIES

SECRETS of CHOCOLATE

Deep in the jungle of South America, where the mighty Amazon River feeds more than two million square miles (5.2 million sq km) of rain forest, there is a strange tree. One-foot (30-cm)-long bright yellow pods cling to its branches, looking like something that might hatch aliens. But inside them is something else, something that gives the tree its name: cacao, meaning "food of the gods" in Greek. This is a chocolate tree.

People have been obsessed with chocolate for 4,000 years. Ancient people thought it was so special that they even used it as money! What are the secrets that make it the most popular sweet on the planet?

Bitter Beginnings

Chocolate can be traced back to the Maya and Aztec, people who lived throughout Mexico and Central America until the 16th century. But they didn't eat it—they drank it! One Aztec legend tells of a feathered serpent god called Quetzalcoatl, who brought cacao beans from paradise. He taught the people how to make a drink called *chocolatl* from the beans. The other gods thought the chocolate drink was too good for humans to enjoy, so when they found out what Quetzalcoatl had done, they were furious! As punishment, they chased the serpent god out of paradise forever.

The Aztec made chocolatl by roasting cacao beans and grinding them up into a paste that they mixed with water, vanilla, honey, chile peppers, and other spices. This drink didn't taste anything like today's chocolate milk—it was bitter and spicy! But the Aztec believed it was a magical beverage that could cure disease and enhance their moods. The drink was so special they also used it as an offering to the gods. The Maya even worshipped a god of cacao, and only allowed rulers, warriors, priests, and nobles to drink chocolatl.

Sweet History

Spanish conquistadores like Hernán Cortés had gone to Mexico looking for gold and silver, but many brought another treasure home instead— chocolate. The delectable dish first

The Aztec used cacao beans as money.

Every year, more than $75 billion is spent on chocolate worldwide.

made its way out of Central America in 1585 and from there, it spread around the world. Most Europeans didn't even like chocolatl until they swapped the chile pepper in the drink with sugar— and the sweetened beverage became a new craze. By the seventh century, chocolate was a symbol of luxury and wealth, sipped by European nobles.

Chocolate went from beverage to bar in 1828. A Dutchman named Conrad J. van Houten figured out a way to press the fat out of roasted cacao beans, making a cake. That cake could be ground into cocoa powder. Cocoa powder could be mixed into chocolate drinks or combined with sugar and cocoa butter to make chocolate bars and candies. Chocolate-making was

much easier and more affordable as a result, and suddenly the succulent sweet was no longer just a treat for the wealthy.

Science Secrets

Pop a piece of chocolate in your mouth and it begins to melt instantly on your tongue. This delicious property is made possible by a kind of fat called a triglyceride. Different triglycerides melt at different temperatures. That means chocolate makers have to be careful to use exactly the right kind of cocoa and process it perfectly so that the finished product melts in your mouth, but doesn't leave a sticky mess on your fingers. Sounds tough—but at least they get to eat their experiments!

Chocolate might seem sinfully delicious, but some scientists think that it's actually good for you! Dark chocolate has chemicals called flavanols that may help make your heart strong and protect your cells from damage. Of course, too much of anything isn't healthy, so experts say chocolate should only be eaten in small doses. And if you like milk chocolate better than dark, you're out of luck: It has all the butter, fat, and sugar, but none of the health benefits.

The next time you savor a piece of chocolate, consider the thousands of years of art and science that have gone into it. Now that you know the secrets of this decadent dessert, does it taste all the sweeter?

Your **brain** can identify

TASTES

in .0015 second,

faster than the **blink** of an eye.

That's **faster** than your sense of **touch** at .0024 second, or even **vision** at .013 second!

DISCOVER YOUR SECRET SENSING SUPERPOWER!

Go stand in front of the mirror and stick out your tongue. Look closely. What do you see?

The little bumps all over your tongue are covered with taste buds—special cells that sense flavor. They're not just on your tongue: They cover the roof of your mouth, the back of your throat, and there are even some inside your nose! They can sense five basic tastes: sweet, sour, salty, bitter, and savory. The flavor of food comes from a combination of these tastes, plus the aromas that you smell while you're eating. (That's why food tastes less flavorful when you're sick.)

Your taste buds make food taste good. But they're also your body's warning system. If your taste buds sense a toxic flavor, they can let your brain know in just .0015 second. That way, you can spit out the poisonous food and stay safe. Thanks, taste buds!

Before a truffle can end up on a plate at a fancy restaurant, it has to be found in the forest—no easy task, since the fungus that produces them grows underground. For centuries, human truffle hunters used pigs to help them.

Why do humans use pigs to hunt for truffles?

THE EXPERT: Charles Lefevre, a mycologist, or mushroom scientist

Q WHY ARE PIGS TRADITIONALLY USED TO FIND TRUFFLES?

A: Different kinds of truffles have different kinds of animals that spread their spores. The famous European truffles—the world's most expensive—are spread by wild pigs. Pigs have a great sense of smell, and they find food by rooting around in the soil with their noses. So pigs already know how to look for truffles. Truffle hunters just strap a leash onto them and go!

Truffles probably evolved, or changed over time, to appeal not just to animals like pigs, but to humans, too. In the part of France where truffles are found, there are caves that humans have lived in for 100,000 years. In that stretch of time, truffles have grown and changed to attract us to eat them. Our noses are really good at detecting the chemicals that make up a truffle's smell.

Q FIRST OF ALL, WHAT EXACTLY IS A TRUFFLE?

A: Truffles are mushrooms. Every family of mushroom has at least one truffle member. There are probably a thousand species of truffles in North America alone. A few of these are culinary truffles—truffles that people eat.

Truffle mushrooms grow underground, on the roots of trees. The part that we eat is the fruit of the mushroom. Just like the apple of an apple tree, a truffle is tasty because it wants to be eaten. That's because it depends on animals to spread its spores, or seeds. So truffles produce a smell that attracts animals to find them and eat them.

Truffles are the world's most expensive food. In 2016, a 4.2-pound (1.9-kg) white truffle sold for $61,250.

Q ARE THERE ANY OTHER WAYS OF FINDING TRUFFLES?

A: Yes. Actually, the most ancient method of searching for truffles—other than just smelling them out yourself—was to use truffle flies. These are flies that lay their eggs on the truffles. People would watch for where these flies were landing on the ground in groups. They would dig there. People in France use this method to this day.

But the most common modern way of finding truffles is dogs. Pigs are great at it, but the problem is they like to eat the truffles. And if you've ever met a pig, you know that they pretty much do whatever they want! Dogs are much easier to handle.

There's another big advantage to dogs. Truffles are so rare and so expensive that truffle hunters are very secretive. They don't want to give away their spots. If someone is out in the woods with a pig on a leash, everyone knows what she's doing. If someone is out in the forest with a dog, she just looks like somebody walking her dog—but she could be a secret truffle hunter!

STRAWBERRIES AREN'T BERRIES.

Berries have their seeds on the inside. Strawberries don't. They're technically a false fruit, and their true fruits are the little brown flecks we call seeds that dot their bright red flesh.

FUNKY FRUIT

BANANAS HAVE SEEDS.

If you've ever noticed little black dots inside your breakfast banana, you've spotted its seeds. But those spots are actually immature seeds that will never develop. Commercial bananas were bred that way. If you were to peel a wild banana, you'd find lots of big seeds that would make the fruit hard to eat.

DO YOU THINK YOU HAVE FRUIT ALL FIGURED OUT? READ ON. THESE STRANGE SECRETS MAY JUST THROW YOU FOR A LOOP. ONE THING'S FOR SURE—YOU'LL NEVER LOOK AT THE PRODUCE AISLE THE SAME WAY AGAIN.

CRANBERRIES AREN'T GROWN UNDERWATER.

You may have seen commercials that show cranberry farmers wading through their fields. But that's not exactly how it works. Cranberries have air pockets inside them that make them float. So when it's time to harvest, farmers flood the fields for easy picking.

TOMATOES ARE THE MOST POPULAR FRUIT IN THE WORLD.

They're another sneaky fruit that seems like a vegetable. And they're also the world's best seller, with more than 60 million tons (54.4 million t) produced each year.

MANY PLANTS AREN'T GROWN FROM SEEDS.

Think about it—what exactly are the farmers planting to grow a seedless orange? The answer: They're not planting, they're grafting. If a farmer wants to plant a seedless orange, he cuts a branch from an existing seedless orange tree, then attaches the cut branch to the branch of another tree. The cut branch will sprout seedless oranges. In this way, farmers can make one tree produce several varieties of fruit.

AVOCADOS ARE ACTUALLY BERRIES.

We usually think of fruits as sweet. But creamy, savory avocados are technically fruits—with their fleshy pulp and their seed on the inside, they're considered a kind of berry.

NOT ALL ORANGES ARE ORANGE.

Orange skin contains chlorophyll, the same chemical compound that makes leaves green. In warm, sunny countries, the chlorophyll stays in the fruit. It's only when oranges are exposed to cold that the chlorophyll breaks down and the fruit turns the familiar orange color. In South American countries and tropical countries near the Equator, it doesn't get cold enough for this to happen. There, oranges stay green all year round!

SECRETS ▶▶▶▶▶ of CHILE

You're chowing down on some tasty tacos when—oh no!—it hits you. Fire seems to fill your mouth. Your face turns red, your eyes water, and you start to cough. You grab for your glass, but water doesn't tame the flames. You've swallowed a spicy chile pepper, and now you're feeling the burn.

But how can a food make you feel like your mouth is on fire? And what can you do to stop the sensation?

Warming Up

When we drink something hot like tea or cocoa, special cells in our mouth signal the brain that what we're eating is hot. Chiles have a chemical compound called capsaicin that triggers those same cells. Cue the sweating and burning feeling.

"Chile peppers became spicy to trick mammals into not eating them," says Paul Bosland, director of The Chile Pepper Institute at New Mexico State University. "That's because when mammals—including humans—eat chile peppers, their digestive systems destroy the seeds." And like all plants, chiles need to spread their seeds so they can grow more chiles.

But birds' digestive systems are different. Unlike mammals, birds poop out chile seeds unharmed. And because birds fly long distances, they can spread seeds far. For the chile pepper, getting eaten by a bird is a very good thing. So the capsaicin that makes our mouth catch on fire doesn't affect birds: They can't taste it! Birds can eat spicy chiles, no sweat.

Hot, Hot, Hot

If chile peppers are designed to taste unpleasant to humans, why do some people love eating them? Chile peppers originally grew in Mexico, Bosland explained. When humans came to the area 20,000 years ago, they probably used the potent plants as medicine. "The Aztec even wrote that chile

Red chile pepper is the number one red food coloring component in the world. It's even used in candies and lipstick.

PEPPERS

peppers cured toothaches," says Bosland. "The sensation of heat makes your body produce pain-blocking chemicals. So they really did work!"

Over time, humans got used to the taste. Those same pain-blocking chemicals that can soothe a sore tooth also give us a rush, just like riding a roller coaster, says Bosland. Some people get a kick out of that daredevil sensation. But not everyone can take the heat. Some people have more heat sensors, some fewer. So if you can tolerate more hot tacos than your friend, you might have a less sensitive mouth. "It's very rare, but there are even people who have no heat receptors at all. They're

like birds," says Bosland.

It's not all about heat. There are more than 1,000 different chemical compounds in chile peppers. Different peppers get their flavors from different combinations of these compounds. Even the type of heat differs, says Bosland. "Some heat feels sharp like pins. Or it might feel flat, like it was painted on with a paintbrush. It can happen fast or slow; it can feel like a tingle on your lips or a fire in the back of your throat."

FIRE!
What do you do if you can't handle the heat? The capsaicin that makes peppers spicy is only found in the white

strings of tissue inside the pepper. Cut those out, and you'll get rid of most of the heat.

But sometimes it's too late, and you've already eaten something so spicy you can't handle it. If your mouth is on fire, reach for the milk, says Bosland. A protein in milk will block the capsaicin from reaching your heat sensors, dulling the sensation. Whatever you do, don't drink water, he says. It might put out a real fire, but it won't do anything for the one in your mouth.

WHY DO YOU FEEL SLEEPY AFTER A BIG MEAL?

It's Thanksgiving and you've just polished off your third helping of turkey, mashed potatoes, and gravy. You stumble over to the couch to watch the football game. Minutes later, your eyes are closed and you're breathing deeply. You're in a food coma—that feeling of extreme sleepiness after you eat a big meal.

SLEEP SCIENCE

This post-meal sleepiness has long mystified scientists. But in 2016, they got some new insight behind the phenomenon. A team of researchers from several Florida, U.S.A., universities fed fruit flies a big meal, and then watched what happened. They found that certain foods caused the flies to get sleepy while others didn't. Flies that ate protein settled in for a 40-minute snooze. Flies that ate sugar didn't seem to need a nap.

Then the team decided to see what was going on in the flies' brains during their food-caused slumber. They found that eating protein activated a certain set of brain cells, which caused the flies to go to sleep. When the researchers shut off these neurons, the flies didn't get sleepy—even after chowing down on the insect equivalent of Thanksgiving dinner.

We spend about one-third of our lives asleep.

MORE MYSTERIES

The mystery of the food coma still isn't totally solved. Scientists don't know why protein makes flies sleep. And they still have no idea why creatures sleep after eating in the first place. In the wild, sleep is risky: A predator could easily attack while an animal is snoring away. Sleep must have some really important function to make it worth the risk of being eaten. But what?

Scientists have come up with a few theories for why we might sleep. Some think that sleep helps us form memories. While we snooze, our brains decide what information we learned that day is worth keeping—and what isn't. It converts important data from short-term memories, which fade quickly away, into long-term memories, which stay with us forever. Other scientists think that sleep is the brain's time to clean house. They found that during slumber, fluid travels around the brain, clearing waste chemicals. Still others think that sleep simply helps us save energy.

Whatever the reason for sleep, it seems strange that the act of eating would make us nod off. Researchers hope to keep working until they crack the case of the food coma. Let's just hope they don't try it after a big meal!

SLEEP CYCLE

STAGE 1

STAGE 2

STAGE 3

REM SLEEP

Stage 1:
This is when a person begins to drift off. If someone is woken up during this stage, they might not even know they were sleeping.

Stage 2:
During this sleep stage, the heart and breathing rates slow down, and the body relaxes.

Stage 3:
Brain waves slow and the body enters deep sleep. Someone woken up from stage 3 sleep will feel very groggy and disoriented.

REM Sleep:
After going through all three sleep stages, the person enters REM sleep. It's short for Rapid Eye Movement, because the eyes move from side to side underneath their eyelids. This is the stage when dreaming occurs.

NUMBERS
UNCOVERED

We live our lives surrounded by numbers, without thinking twice about them. But all kinds of strange secrets are hiding in the facts, stats, and digits we encounter every day. For example, did you know that a frog can use its sticky tongue to grab prey in just seven hundredths of a second? That's faster than a viper strikes. Or that there's a moon in the solar system with volcanoes that shoot 190 miles (300 km) high? That's taller than 34 Mount Everests stacked on top of each other! This chapter holds more than 30 surprising facts and shocking secrets about numbers ... but who's counting?

Sixty tons (54 t) of SPACE DUST falls to Earth each day.

WHAT'S UP WITH THIS COSMIC CLUTTER?

The next time your dad asks you to sweep the porch, think about this: The dust you're cleaning is made up of teeny pieces of dirt, leaves, and even dead skin cells (eww!). But that's not all ... some of it comes from space.

Scientists have known about cosmic dust for a long time. It's made of very small bits like little chunks of meteors, debris from comet collisions, and leftovers from the formation of the planets. This star stuff floats through the universe, and some of it lands on Earth. But until 2015, scientists had no idea just how much space dust we're dealing with each day. Then they measured the ingredients in our atmosphere and found the shocking answer: 60 tons (54 t)—the weight of about five school buses! If all that cosmic dust makes you want to get out your broom, think again: It helps form our clouds and also feeds tiny sea-dwelling plankton in Antarctica.

COOL CASH

YOU KNOW IT CAN BUY YOUR LUNCH AND FEED THE PARKING METER.
But there's a lot about the bills and coins you carry that might surprise you.
Read on to discover some strange secrets about money.

FLOWER FOOD

Outdated and torn bills have to be retired. In the past, they were cut up or burned. But today, they don't become either trash or ash: Banks and individuals hand them over, and then a farm in Delaware, U.S.A., mulches more than four tons (3.6 t) of cash into compost each day. That's some fancy fertilizer!

MAKING CENTS

Metal costs more than it used to. Since 2006, the United States Mint has had to spend more to make pennies and nickels than the coins are worth. It now costs about 1.7 cents to create a penny and 8 cents to make a nickel. That just doesn't make cents!

HIGH TECH

The $100 bill is equipped with the spiffiest anti-counterfeiting technology of any U.S. bill: It comes with a 3-D security ribbon woven into the fabric. If you look at it while tilting your head back and forth, you'll see the bells on the note change to 100s. This makes the bill very hard to fake.

FOLD ME

These days, money is made to last. It takes an average of 8,000 folds to tear a bill. Though bills are nicknamed "paper money," they're actually made of cloth. In Ben Franklin's time, people used to sew up tears in their bills with needle and thread.

CREATIVE CURRENCY

Before bills and coins, ancient people used some odd objects as currency. Items used as money throughout history include salt, squirrel pelts, potato mashers, shells, and tea. Today, one bank in Modena, Italy, accepts Parmesan cheese as collateral for loans to help cheesemakers get through lean times. The bank loan lasts up to 34 months—the exact amount of time it takes the cheese to age.

A frog's
TONGUE
can snag prey in .07 second—

five times faster than a human blinks!

THAT'S ONE AGILE APPENDAGE!

One day in 2017, a group of frog scientists in Atlanta, Georgia, U.S.A., were passing the time online when they came across a video of a large frog called a Pacman frog doing something unusual. While a human helper held a phone, the frog was playing a game on the screen! The object of the game was to tap moving bugs to earn points. Human thumbs are pretty good at this, but the frog's tongue was even better. That made the scientists wonder—what exactly makes the frog so skilled?

First, the scientists used high-speed video cameras to catch frogs in action. They found that the frog sends its tongue flying toward its insect prey at incredible speeds. Its tongue accelerates at 12 times the force of gravity. For comparison, astronauts reach three times the force of gravity during a rocket launch! If you think a big bug might be hard to swallow in one gulp, you're right! The frog gets an assist from its eyeballs, which squeeze downward into its head to help push the food down its throat. Yum!

Marvelous MOONS

Jupiter has a total of 69 weird, wild, and wonderful moons. Most of them are still mysteries to science. Here's an up-close look at the secrets behind a few of Jupiter's most spectacular satellites.

Io

One of the strangest objects in the solar system, Io is completely covered with huge volcanoes. They spew fountains of sulfur 190 miles (300 km) into the atmosphere. It's one of just a handful of places in the solar system that are known to have volcanic activity.

EUROPA

The lines on Europa are cracks in its surface, which is made entirely of ice. Scientists think that below the ice, Europa probably has an ocean bigger than Earth's—and there's a chance alien life could be swimming there. NASA hopes to send a probe to fly by the planet to learn more in the 2020s.

GANYMEDE

At 3,273 miles (5,268 km) across, this is the largest moon in the solar system. It's bigger than the planet Mercury! It's the only known moon in the solar system to have a magnetic field. Scientists think that like Europa, Ganymede could be home to a hidden ocean.

LEDA

At just 11 miles (18 km) across, Leda is the smallest moon in the solar system. Some astronomers think it was created when an asteroid came so close to Jupiter that the planet's gravity pulled it in and broke it up into pieces. One of those pieces became Leda.

METIS

The closest moon to Jupiter, Metis, whizzes by only 79,598 miles (128,100 km) above the planet's surface. It's so close that scientists know it will eventually crash into its parent planet.

CALLISTO

Since it was formed 4.5 billion years ago, Callisto has been getting hammered by flying rocks called meteors. Today, its surface is covered with marks and scars from the impacts. It has more craters than any other object in the solar system.

Police dogs sniff out crime with their seriously impressive sense of smell: A bloodhound can follow scents that are 300 hours, or more than 12 days, old.

How can a
bloodhound follow
an old scent trail?

THE EXPERT: Gopikrishna Deshpande is a bioengineer at Auburn University in Alabama, U.S.A., who studies how dogs' brains process smells.

Q HOW DOES THE SENSE OF SMELL WORK?

A dog has up to 300 million smell receptors in its nose. That's 50 times more than humans have!

A: Smell is just a combination of certain chemicals. Once those chemicals are inside the nose, they go into a structure between the nose and the brain called the olfactory bulb. This bulb has all kinds of sensors. Different ones respond to different chemicals.

Suppose you are smelling an orange. When the chemicals that make that citrus smell hit the right sensors, the sensors send out electrical signals. The brain reads those signals and deduces that you're smelling citrus.

Q HOW CAN BLOODHOUNDS SENSE A SMELL THAT IS 300 HOURS OLD?

A: Dogs have a much bigger olfactory bulb than humans—about 40 times bigger, relative to the size of their brain! The olfactory bulb takes up one-eighth of a dog's brain. That means that dogs have far more smell sensors than humans. Their sense of smell is at least a thousand times better than ours.

When a scent is old—like the smell of a person who has passed by many hours before—the chemicals that make the scent have mostly drifted away. But some of them are still there. Our noses can't detect them, but a bloodhound's nose can.

Scent travels up a dog's nostrils to the smell receptors, or sensors, at the back of its nose.

Q HOW DO HUMANS USE A DOG'S SENSE OF SMELL TO HELP US?

A: Dogs are a huge help to law enforcement officers. With their sensitive noses, they can sniff out dangerous substances or help find missing people. Years ago, one group of scientists tried to make an artificial nose that could do these tasks as well as a canine officer. But they didn't even come close. That's how incredible a dog's nose is!

The smell receptors send signals to the dog's brain. There, the olfactory bulb makes sense of the information to figure out what the scent is.

WHEN YOU LOOK AT THE STARS, YOU'RE LOOKING INTO THE PAST.

Light is fast—the fastest thing in the universe. But it still takes time to reach us. It takes 8.6 years for light from Sirius, the brightest star in the sky, to travel to Earth. So we see the star as it was 8.6 years ago. If Sirius exploded today, we wouldn't know for another 8.6 years!

ODD FACTS ABOUT TIME

WHEN YOU'RE WAITING FOR LUNCHTIME, THE CLOCK SEEMS TO SLOW DOWN. EVERY MINUTE FEELS LIKE IT TAKES AN HOUR TO TICK BY. THEN WHEN YOU'RE EATING AND CHATTING WITH YOUR FRIENDS, IT SEEMS LIKE YOU BLINK AND LUNCHTIME'S OVER! BUT TIME IS EVEN WEIRDER THAN YOU THINK.

THE UNIVERSE IS 13.8 BILLION YEARS OLD.

If we compressed all that time into a year, life would first appear on September 22. *T. rex* would walk the Earth on December 28. Humans wouldn't appear until 11:54 p.m. on that day, and they wouldn't invent the wheel until just fifteen seconds before midnight.

A YEAR DOESN'T LAST 356 DAYS.

Yep, go ahead and correct your science teacher: A year actually lasts 365.2422 days—that's how long it takes the Earth to go around the sun. About every four years, we add a day to the year to make up for it—those are leap years. Even the ancient Egyptians did this!

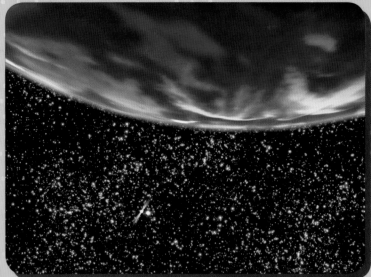

THE OLDEST KNOWN PLANET IS MORE THAN TWICE AS OLD AS EARTH.

Nicknamed the Genesis planet, it's 2.5 times bigger than Jupiter and 5,600 light-years away. Astronomers estimate it was formed about 13 billion years ago, making it almost as old as the universe itself.

WHEN DINOSAURS LIVED, A DAY LASTED 21 HOURS.

All objects in space have gravity, a pulling force. The moon's gravity pulls on Earth, slowing the planet's spin. It only slows us by about a 500th of a second every century—but over billions of years, that adds up, making our days longer!

THE WORLD'S OLDEST LIVING TREE IS 9,550 YEARS OLD.

Called Old Tjikko, it may not look very impressive. But this tree, discovered in the Dalarna province in Sweden, sprouted up during the end of the last Ice Age, when woolly mammoths walked the Earth.

Army ants swarm in colonies of up to half a million.

ASTOUNDING ANTS

SECRETS of a MEGACOLONY

You might notice ants when they make a trail across your kitchen counter, or suddenly appear all over your sandwich at a picnic. Other than that, you probably don't give them too much thought. But you should—because ants are taking over the world.

Scientists have known for a long time that ants live in colonies—huge groups that work together to hunt for food, build nests, and fight off predators. In 2010, scientists discovered that one species, Argentine ants, forms one extended family. Though these ants are separated by oceans, they make up one giant megacolony that reaches across the entire planet.

Starting Small
The ants in a colony work together to survive and grow their numbers. They can cooperate to accomplish incredible tasks, like moving a millipede many times their size, or grabbing on to each other to form a living raft that will float on floodwaters.

The most important member of an ant colony is the queen. She's the mother of every other ant. The queen can lay up to 1,000 eggs a day for years. She raises her babies until they're a month old, when they're ready to start working. These worker ants head out of the nest to search for food, like insects and seeds, to feed the next generation of babies.

By themselves, ants aren't very smart. But ants can think as a group, solving complex problems like choosing the best nesting site together. Ants are so committed to the colony that they'll give their own lives to protect it. They're so united that scientists now think that an ant colony actually behaves like a single creature, called a superorganism.

Thinking Big
Argentine ants are known for their appetites: These ants won't stop at your sandwich; they'll eat anything, from meat to candy to vegetable oil. Unlike many other ant species, Argentine ant colonies can have many queens. That means that their colony can get really big, really fast. When one colony gets too big, some of the ants split off and head out into the wilderness to find a new home.

When two ants meet, they'll sniff each other with their antennae, says Ellen van Wilgenburg, an entomologist, or insect scientist, at Fordham University in New York City. Ants from the same colony recognize each other

Weaver ants can lift 100 times their own weight.

Bull ants can be an inch and a half (38 mm) long.

ANTS AT WORK

You probably thought only humans could do some of these jobs. But teeny tiny ants aren't so different from us after all.

Farmer Ants: Leaf-cutter ant larvae can only eat one thing, a special kind of fungus called Lepiotaceae. So the ants are farmers that grow this fungus in their nests. Every day, workers head out to chomp off plant chunks. They carry the plant material back to the nest and feed it to the fungus. They care for their fungus crop, keeping it free of pests and mold. When it's big enough, they harvest it and feed it to their young.

Pirate Ants: These ants don't raise their own youngsters. Instead, they invade other nests, raid their nurseries, and steal their larvae. When these larvae hatch, the pirate ants put them to work as babysitters. The stolen ants bring up the pirate ants' babies.

Artist Ants: Weaver ants' nests aren't just homes, they're works of art. The ants pull leaves close to each other and then "weave" them together with a silk they collect from their larvae.

Attack Ants: Most ant species use their sensitive antennae to get around by smell. Not bull ants. Ellen van Wilgenburg warns, "They'll see you from a meter [3 feet] away, and if you're near their nest, they'll run after you!"

by a "signature" of chemicals they all carry. "If they're from the same colony, they'll continue on with their business. But if they're from different colonies, they'll fight and maybe even kill each other," she says. Argentine ants are especially aggressive.

Super Bugs

Van Wilgenburg wanted to study the relationships between different Argentine ants from around the world. She collected ants from California, Japan, Europe, and other places. Then she put them head-to-head and waited for the battle to begin.

To her surprise, the ants didn't fight. Just like ants from the same family, they would sniff each other and walk away peacefully. Van Wilgenburg found that these ants all carry very similar chemical signatures—even

though they were from supercolonies on different continents. She checked out their genes, and discovered that they were closely related. "They're like one big family," she says.

This makes one massive megacolony of ants that spans Asia, Australia, New Zealand, Japan, Europe, and the Americas. The strangest part about all these ants, van Wilgenburg says, is that humans made it possible. Argentine ants once lived only in South America. But around 1882, some of them probably hitched a ride on a boat and landed in Madeira, Spain, a major trade center. From there, they went on to global domination. Today, the megacolony has invaded every continent except Antarctica.

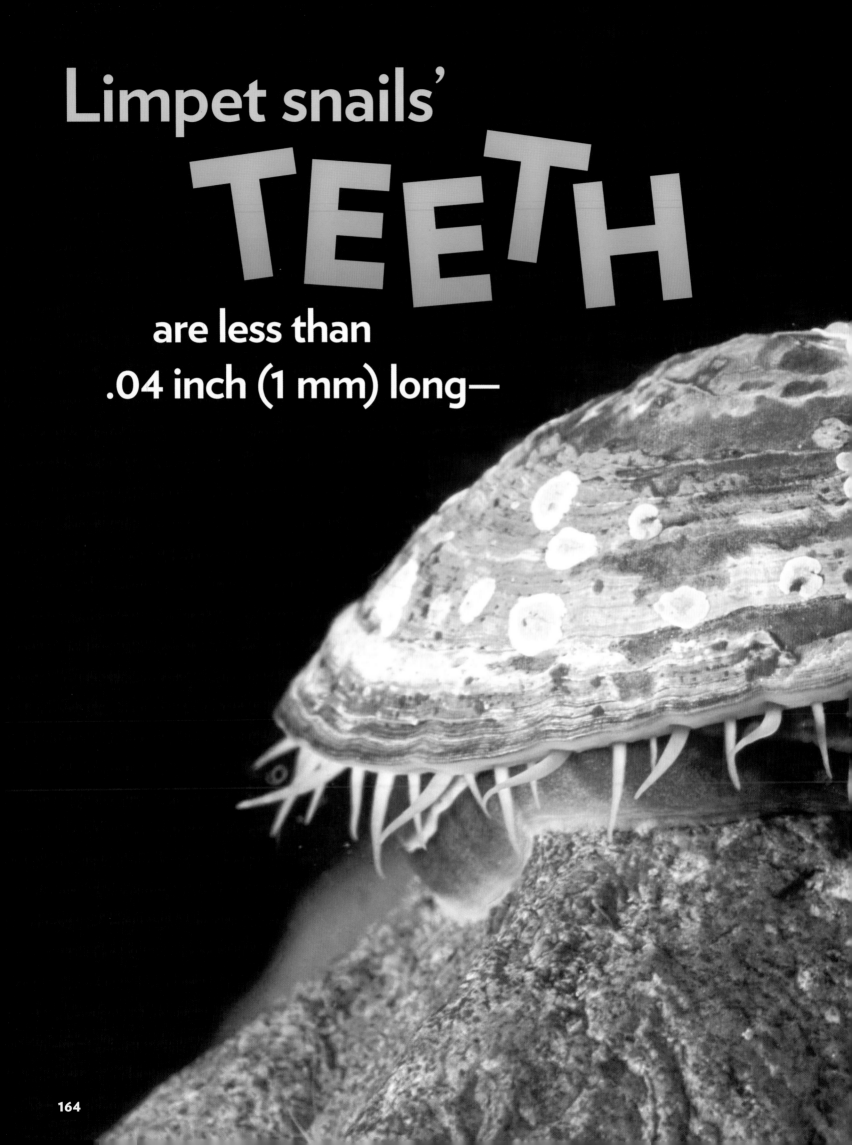

Limpet snails' **TEETH** are less than .04 inch (1 mm) long—

but they're stronger than titanium.

THESE TINY TEETH MAKE FOR A MIGHTY MOUTH!

What's the strongest material in the natural world? For a long time, scientists thought it was spider silk, which is stronger than steel. But in 2017, they discovered a new contender: the teeth of the limpet, a type of snail that lives underwater.

Like you, limpets use their thousands of teeth for eating. But their favorite food isn't pizza or ice cream. Limpets eat by scraping the algae off of rocks. While they're feeding, they chomp away at the stone like tiny bulldozers. If you ate rocks, your teeth would be ground to bits in no time. But researchers who studied the limpet's teeth found that it would take a lot of force to break them—about the same amount that turns carbon into diamonds deep inside the Earth! These snail chompers are 40 percent stronger than the strongest spider silk. The scientists think we could someday copy the limpet's tooth to make superstrong materials.

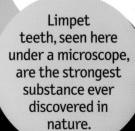

Limpet teeth, seen here under a microscope, are the strongest substance ever discovered in nature.

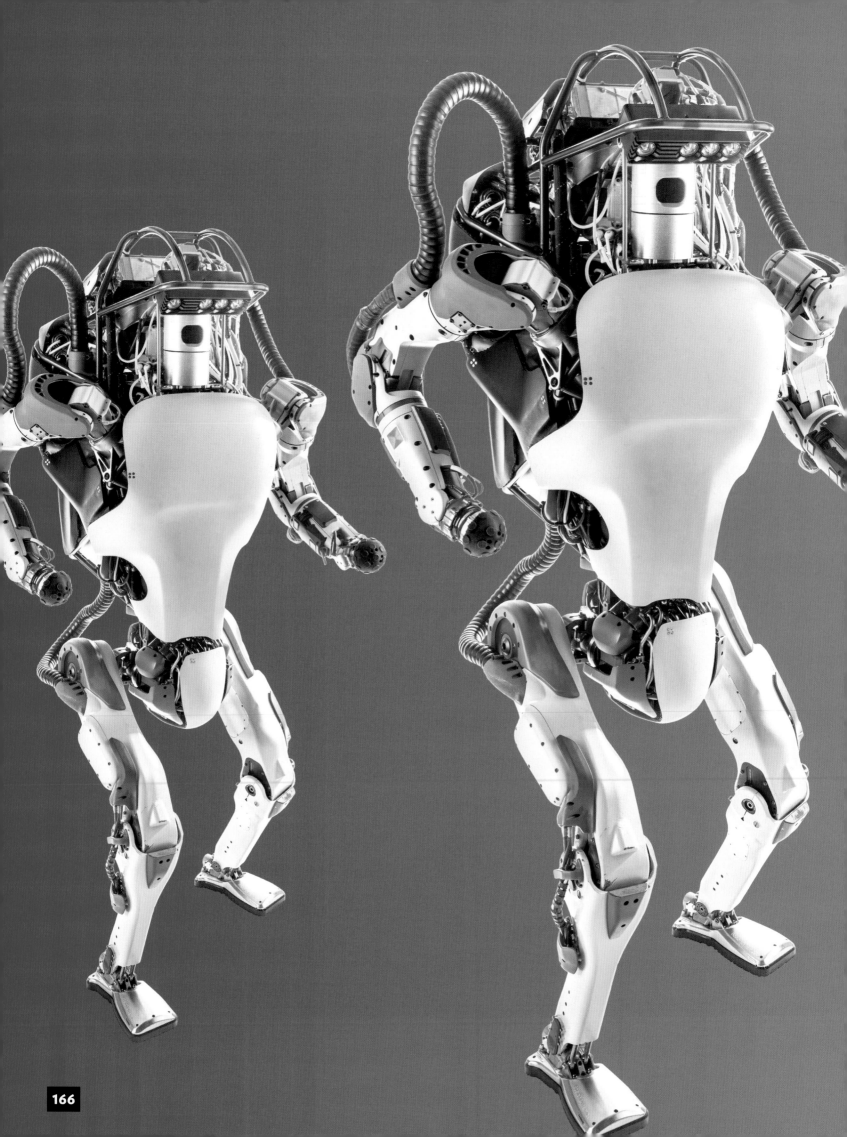

EYE-OPENING
INVENTIONS

You might know the Wright brothers made their sky-high dreams come true when they came up with the first airplane. You may have heard that Alexander Graham Bell invented the telephone. But you won't find the following inventors and their creations in your history books. Read on to learn the strange-but-true origins of everyday objects, from microwaves to memory foam. And dive into the hidden mysteries of the world's coolest new gadgets, from a robot that can drive to virtual-reality goggles!

The TRAMPOLINE

was invented by a 16-year-old boy ...

who had a kangaroo

help him test it!

THIS INVENTOR HOPPED RIGHT INTO HISTORY!

In 1930 a teenager named George Nissen ran away with the circus. Well, not exactly—but when the traveling circus came to his town, Cedar Rapids, Iowa, U.S.A., Nissen was captivated by the sight of the trapeze artists finishing their death-defying routines by dropping into a safety net below. It gave him an idea—what if instead of a safety net, they could fall into something that would let them keep on bouncing and flipping?

Nissen started tinkering in his parents' garage. With the help of his high school gymnastics coach, he created a bouncing device out of scrap metal and tire inner tubes. With a boost from his "bouncing rig," Nissen was able to leap into a back somersault. Nissen named his invention after the Spanish word for diving board: *el trampolín*, and he devoted the rest of his life to getting the word out. In 1960, he decided he needed a promotional photo that would amaze potential customers. So he enlisted the help of a bouncing expert—a kangaroo named Victoria! Nissen taught her how to hop on the trampoline, and the photo of the acrobatic inventor and his animal assistant helped make the trampoline famous around the world.

NISSEN

WI-FI

If you picture an eyeglass-wearing tech genius when you think about the invention of Wi-Fi, you're way off. The creator behind the system that powers modern computers and cell phone networks was actually a glamorous actress named Hedy Lamarr. Beautiful and talented, she was one of the most popular actresses around during the golden age of movies, from the late 1920s to the early 1960s. But after a day spent on set, Lamarr would head not to a Hollywood party, but to her private laboratory. There, she tinkered with creations ranging from a fluorescent dog collar to modifications for the Concorde airplane. Her most famous invention of all was a torpedo guidance system that went on to become our modern Wi-Fi and cell phone networks.

SURPRISING STORIES OF EVERYDAY STUFF

YOU MIGHT THINK THERE'S NOT MUCH MYSTERY INVOLVED IN SQUEEZING SOME KETCHUP ONTO YOUR HOT DOG, OR CONNECTING A COMPUTER TO THE LIBRARY'S WI-FI. THINK AGAIN. THESE EVERYDAY ITEMS, FROM A FAVORITE TOY TO A MACHINE FOR CATCHING CRIMINALS, ARE HIDING CRAZY HISTORIES. SOME WERE INVENTED BY PEOPLE WHO ARE FAMOUS FOR OTHER THINGS ENTIRELY; OTHERS ARE JUST PLAIN ODD.

THE SCRAPBOOK

When you think of scrapbooks, you might picture yourself armed with stickers, glitter, and a rainbow of markers. So, the scrapbook's inventor couldn't be more unlikely: gray-haired, sharp-tongued author Mark Twain. Twain had a secret second life as an inventor. His creations include a replacement for suspenders and a history trivia game. But his scrapbook was his most famous creation. Tired of using glue to stick down his mementos to paper, he came up with something better in 1872: a scrapbook that already had glue on the pages, like a postage stamp. To stick down a souvenir, you just had to lick the page.

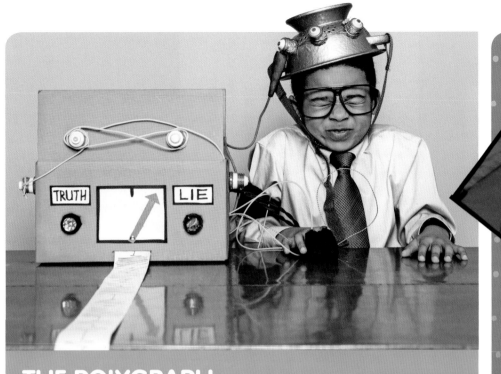

THE POLYGRAPH

The mastermind behind Wonder Woman—the most famous superheroine of all time—was William Marston, a psychologist who wrote comics on the side. But that's not all he invented, Marston was also the creator of technology that led to the lie detector test. Marston first started tinkering with a type of blood pressure test in 1915 that went on to become part of the polygraph (nicknamed the lie detector test) still used by real-life crime fighters today. And it also made many cameos in Marston's Wonder Woman comics—as Wonder Woman's favorite weapon: the Lasso of Truth.

KETCHUP

Ketchup is a condiment made with tomatoes ... right? Well, it wasn't always. The thick red sauce gets its name from a Chinese sauce called *ke-tsiap*, made of fermented fish. That might sound hard to swallow, but Dutch and English sailors got a taste for the stuff, and tried to re-create it at home with walnuts, celery, mushrooms, and other ingredients at hand. But early ketchup didn't keep very well—in 1866 a French cookbook author described it as "filthy, decomposed, and putrid." Ketchup got a modern makeover when a man named Henry J. Heinz discovered that tomatoes acted as a natural preservative when added to the recipe. Today, more than 650 million bottles of Heinz ketchup are sold worldwide each year.

KITES

Today, people travel to the beach or park to fly a kite just for the joy of watching this colorful contraption swoop through the air. But kites used to be much more serious. They first originated in China around 1000 B.C. as military signals—their colors, patterns, and maneuvers were used as codes to pass along information to nearby troops. Han dynasty soldiers outfitted kites with bamboo pipes that made a frightening whistling noise when flown over the enemy. Other ancient Chinese troops used giant kites that could carry a soldier, like an early version of spy planes. What's lost to history? Who was fearless enough to sign up for that job!

ROBOT Revolution

This robot may look like a science fiction character, but it's not: This is a real robot called Atlas.

Invented by robotics company Boston Dynamics, it's one of the most advanced robots in the world.

BIONIC BRAIN

Atlas has three onboard computers that help it navigate the world around it and plan its next moves. A wireless router in its head allows it to communicate with a human team.

LASER VISION

Atlas may look like a human, but it one-ups us in the sight department. The robot has two vision systems: One is a set of cameras, and the other is a laser range finder. It works by shooting out laser beams that bounce off the robot's surroundings. Atlas's computers analyze how the beams bounce back to figure out what's around it.

CYBORG STATS

At 5 feet 9 inches (1.75 m) and 180 pounds (82 kg), Atlas is about the size of an average human man. That allows the robot to go where humans go and do what they do—like climb a ladder or connect a fire hose to a hydrant.

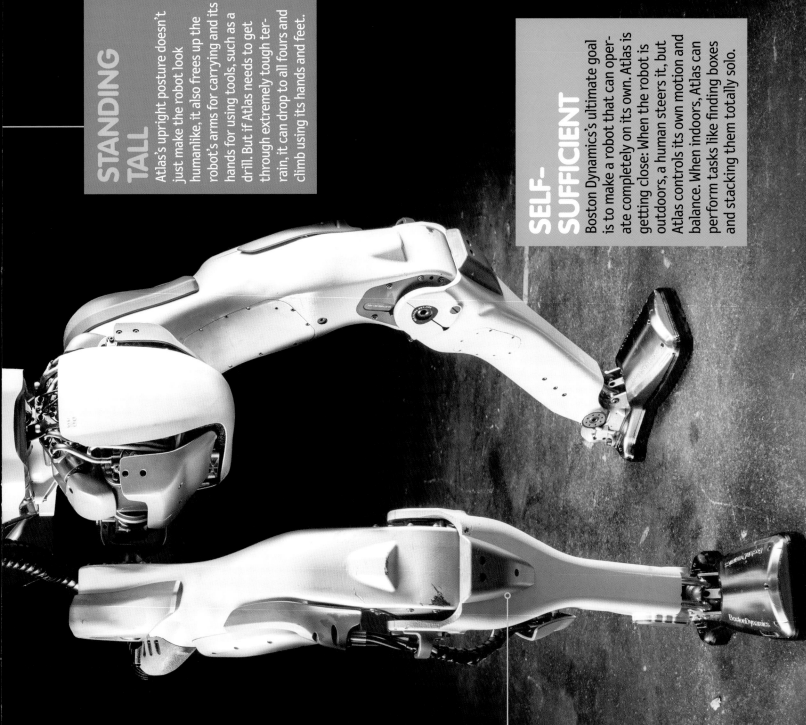

STANDING TALL

Atlas's upright posture doesn't just make the robot look humanlike, it also frees up the robot's arms for carrying and its hands for using tools, such as a drill. But if Atlas needs to get through extremely tough terrain, it can drop to all fours and climb using its hands and feet.

SELF-SUFFICIENT

Boston Dynamics's ultimate goal is to make a robot that can operate completely on its own. Atlas is getting close: When the robot is outdoors, a human steers it, but Atlas controls its own motion and balance. When indoors, Atlas can perform tasks like finding boxes and stacking them totally solo.

ROBOT UNPLUGGED

Atlas needs a lot of power to run. Old versions had to be plugged into a power source. But the newest Atlas wears a battery pack on its back. The battery provides enough power for Atlas to run totally untethered.

NOT A PUSHOVER

Walking comes easily to humans. But creating a robot that can do it is extremely tough—the Atlas team spent years getting their robot to walk on two legs. Early versions spent a lot of time falling and lying on the ground helplessly until human rescuers gave them a hand. But the newest Atlas is really hard to knock over: In a demonstration, one of the robot's engineers tried—and failed—to push Atlas over with a hockey stick. And if Atlas does fall, the robot can push itself up with its arms and get back on its feet without help.

MECHANICAL

animals roam a French theme park,

some more than 40 feet (12 m) tall—

about the same height as four elephants stacked on top of each other.

WELCOME TO A CREATURE CARNIVAL!

Les Machines de L'île in Nantes, France, is a theme park like no other in the world. It swaps real plants and animals for mechanical ones: half machines, half works of art. You can take a spin on an 82-foot (25-m)-tall carousel that whirls you through the layers of the ocean, from the seafloor to the surface. You can ride inside the abdomen of a spider and on the back of an elephant, which roams the park.

You can even watch the machinists who built the rides at work in the park's laboratory. They're also on hand to explain how their creations work. The park is devoted to the science fiction of Jules Verne, who wrote adventure novels like *Journey to the Center of the Earth* and *20,000 Leagues Under the Sea*. From a rideable giant squid with a 25-foot (8-m) wingspan to a fish with a moving tail to spinning sea creatures, these mechanical animals offer visitors an inside look at nature.

ACCIDENTAL INVENTIONS

SOME OF THE WORLD'S MOST USEFUL INVENTIONS HAVE A SECRET: THEY WEREN'T MADE IN A LAB BY AN INVENTOR WITH WIRY WHITE HAIR. **These creations were invented by accident!** Read on to learn the secrets of turning a slip-up into a success.

CHOCOLATE CHIP COOKIES

Ruth Wakefield, co-owner of the Toll House Inn in Whitman, Massachusetts, U.S.A., was baking for her guests one day when—*uh oh*—she realized she was all out of baker's chocolate. So, she grabbed the closest thing at hand: a bar of semisweet chocolate. She broke the bar up into chunks, stirred them into the batter, and put her cookies in the oven. When the timer dinged, Wakefield pulled out the world's first chocolate chip cookies.

PLAY-DOH

Colorful, moldable Play-Doh didn't start out as a toy. It was meant to be the exact opposite: a cleaning product. A company named Kutol Products invented it to remove soot stains left by coal stoves from wallpaper. That changed when the company discovered that children were using their product for arts and crafts. Kutol removed the cleanser from the recipe, added fun colors, and created one of the most beloved toys of all time.

X-RAY IMAGES

In 1895, a German physicist named Wilhelm Röntgen was experimenting with glass tubes filled with gas called cathode ray tubes. When he ran electricity through the gas, the tubes would glow... but, he noticed, so would a piece of fluorescent cardboard across the room. Röntgen quickly realized that the cathode ray tubes were shooting out invisible x-rays—rays that could pass through paper, wood, and even skin, lighting up the bones beneath.

SLINKY

In 1943, Navy engineer Richard James was trying to come up with a way to keep fragile ship instruments from being knocked over when seas got rough. He was experimenting with a spring-shaped design when he accidentally knocked it off a shelf. To James' amazement, the spring "walked" down a stack of books, onto a table, then to the floor. Realizing he had the perfect toy on his hands, James demonstrated it at a department store in 1945. An hour and a half later, he had sold 400 Slinkys.

SUPERGLUE

Harry Coover, a researcher for the Eastman-Kodak company, was in a sticky situation in 1942. He was trying to come up with a material to create gun sights for soldiers in World War II. But the substance he was experimenting with, cyanoacrylate, wasn't working—it just stuck to everything. Frustrated, Coover abandoned the idea—until 1951, when he realized he had the perfect glue on his hands.

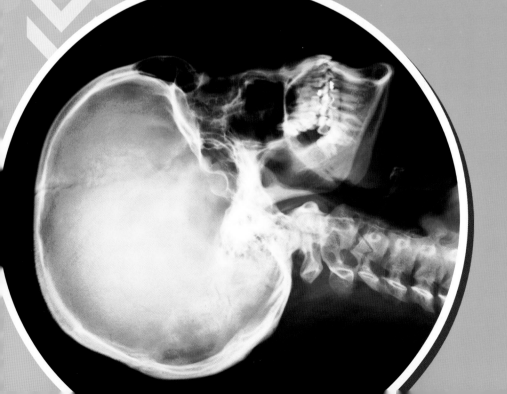

It's 2035, and a space-craft on its way to Mars is crawling with robots. Some scramble straight up its sides; others are upside down, clinging to its belly. They inspect the craft for damage and do repairs. NASA engineers are already on the way to making this scene from science fiction into fact with a climbing robot called LEMUR. This incredible invention can scale sheer walls and was inspired by nature's best climber: the gecko.

How do you invent a **robot** that can climb walls?

THE EXPERT: Aaron Parness, a robotics engineer at NASA's Jet Propulsion Lab in Pasadena, California, U.S.A. Parness leads the team building the bot.

Q HOW DOES A GECKO CLIMB?

A: Geckos are nature's most amazing climbers. They can go from the floor to the ceiling in two seconds. And they can stick to almost anything.

Geckos' climbing secret is these tiny little hairs on the bottoms of their feet. The tips of these hairs are 100 times smaller than the hairs on your head. They stick using a property called Van der Waals forces. Here's what that means: If you get two atoms really close together, they form a bond. It's a very, very weak bond. But the gecko has a ton of hairs on its feet—over one million of them per square millimeter! That means a lot of atoms bonding together, giving the gecko a lot of cling power.

Q HOW DOES YOUR GRIPPER WORK?

A: Our design uses a material that is covered with tiny hairs, just like a gecko's foot. It works really well. Our gripper can grab a 220-pound (100-kg) object and move it around. It can cling to 30 different surfaces and hang on for a year without falling. But we're still only about half as good as the gecko. Nature is still beating us!

Q ARE YOU WORKING ON ANY OTHER CLIMBING ROBOTS?

A: If you look at some of nature's great rock climbers—beetles, grasshoppers, and bears—they don't use tiny hairs like a gecko. Instead, they use claws. So we're working on building claw feet for our LEMUR robot that are covered with hundreds of fishhooks that can grab onto a rock face. These claw feet are like another pair of shoes the robot can switch to for rock climbing.

Wearing its claw feet, the robot could climb Mars's equivalent of the Grand Canyon, called Valles Marineris. If you've ever been to the Grand Canyon, you can see that the rock is made up of many layers. As you go down those layers, you can read back in time to learn what the Earth was like in the past. With our rock-climbing robot, we could do the same thing on Mars!

SuperStadium

Virtual reality (VR):
A computer-generated
experience that makes
you feel as if you're
inside a pretend world

ENTERTAINMENT OF THE FUTURE

Augmented reality (AR): Technology that layers computer-generated images onto things in the real world

A buzzer goes off, marking the start of a race. Your heart is pounding—not that you can hear it over the sound of revving engines. Your car weaves through the other vehicles, making its way to the front of the pack. Your car speeds through the finish line! The crowd roars.

You aren't actually in the car. But thanks to a pair of smart glasses you're wearing in the stands, you experienced exactly what the real driver did on the course.

"In the future, advanced technology will enable us to feel as if we're part of the event," says Aymeric Castaing, founder of Umanimation, a future-tech media company. Read on to get a sneak peek of the ways we'll be entertained by 2060 and beyond!

SUPER STADIUMS

Didn't see that catch? No worries: In the future, 3-D holograms could appear in midair above the field to show replays of sports moments. For some events, you'll even get a seat in a flying pod that can put you close to the action. (The pod even flies you home afterward!) Meanwhile, say goodbye to long lines for food or team jerseys. Through an app, flying drones will deliver anything you order right to your seat.

GAME ON

A colorful alien zooms directly toward you, attempting to knock you aside with its spaceship. You put your hands in front of you, blocking the alien with a powerful force field. As the alien and its crew retreat in defeat, a crowd cheers your dramatic victory.

To the group assembled in front of you in the park, it looks like you're in outer space and just took down an alien in a spaceship—thanks to virtual reality (VR) goggles and a suit with motion sensors that detect your movements. Everything you saw through your goggles was projected onto a video screen at a virtual gaming playground. There, the audience can watch and cheer you on as you go up against the aliens. They can also wear headsets and feel as if they're in outer space, too!

DROID BEATS

Ready to rock out to your favorite band? Whether it's pop-star robots or a robot orchestra conductor, future music may be in nonhuman hands. And audiences won't just hear music played by robots—they'll be able to see it. Augmented reality (AR) glasses will allow audiences to see which notes are coming out of the instruments in front of them. "AR glasses could even enable beginning musicians to take their lessons on the go," Castaing says. "The glasses could essentially become their teacher."

THE BIG SCREEN

There won't be a bad seat in the house at movie theaters in the future. Films will surround the audience with 3-D screens in every direction ... including the floor and ceiling. You'll feel like you're underwater at the latest ocean adventure blockbuster. Plus, robots will deliver the snacks you've ordered from your seat's tablet directly to your rotating chair.

THEY CAME FROM SPACE

SPACE TRAVEL MAY BE FAR OUT—BUT THAT DOESN'T MEAN IT HASN'T CHANGED HOW WE LIVE ON EARTH. NASA scientists have come up with more than 6,000 technologies that are now part of everyday life. You might have used some of them yourself!

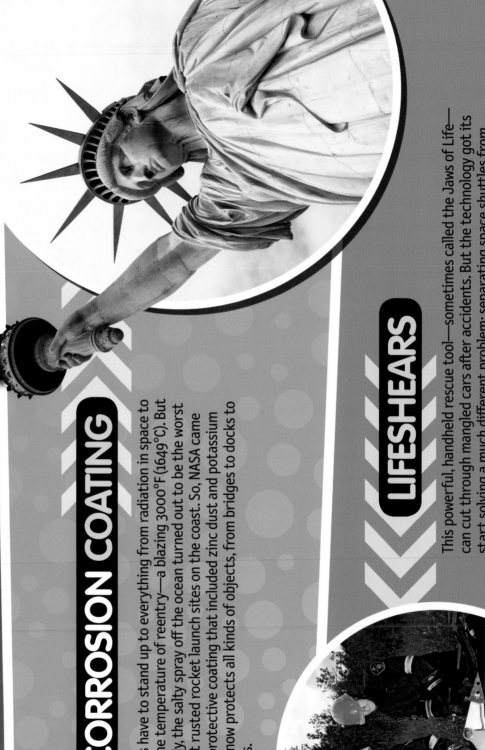

ANTI-CORROSION COATING

Spaceships have to stand up to everything from radiation in space to the extreme temperature of reentry—a blazing 3000°F (1649°C). But surprisingly, the salty spray off the ocean turned out to be the worst offender: It rusted rocket launch sites on the coast. So, NASA came up with a protective coating that included zinc dust and potassium silicate. It now protects all kinds of objects, from bridges to docks to army tanks.

LIFESHEARS

This powerful, handheld rescue tool—sometimes called the Jaws of Life—can cut through mangled cars after accidents. But the technology got its start solving a much different problem: separating space shuttles from their rocket boosters in midair. NASA perfected a type of explosive charge to separate the devices and send their craft skyward. A miniature version powers the life-saving emergency tool.

MEMORY FOAM

Sitting for hours at a time can get uncomfortable—especially if you're a test pilot taking a rough landing. So when NASA asked aeronautical engineer Charles Yost to come up with better airplane seating, he flew at the challenge. Yost invented plastic foam that could de-form under pressure, then spring back to its original shape. Since then, Yost's memory foam has been made into everything from the lining of football players' helmets to mattresses.

INSULIN PUMP

When NASA started thinking about sending astronauts to distant planets, they faced a problem: how to make sure their space travelers stayed healthy. Scientists started working on systems that would allow them to monitor astronauts' vital signs from a control room back on Earth. The invention was adapted to create the insulin pump, a device that can monitor blood sugar and send insulin into the blood when needed. The invention has been saving the lives of diabetics since the late 1980s.

SCRATCH-RESISTANT GLASS

Eyeglasses got their name because until not so long ago, they actually were made of glass. It wasn't the ideal material: It could shatter, sending shards into the wearer's eyes. Plastic offered better optics, but it scratched easily—that is, until a NASA scientist came up with a thin, tough coating meant for spacecraft mechanics. NASA used it to make space helmet visors scratch resistant. After that, it made the leap to Earthlings' eyewear.

183

SECRETS OF
DRONES

Imagine that you're hiking through a field. You stop to admire a flower growing on the side of the trail when you see that you're not the only one interested. A small buzzing creature is zooming around the bloom. But this isn't a bee—it's a tiny flying robot, or drone.

Scientists in Japan are at work developing a bee drone that could pollinate the world's crops. And it's not the only flying robot on the horizon.

LIFTOFF

Some researchers think that drones will help solve problems facing humankind today. Bees currently pollinate about one-third of the world's crops, but the insects are in danger. If drones take over the task, they could help feed the world. In February 2017, researchers at the National Institute of Advanced Industrial Science and Technology in Tokyo attached horsehair coated with a sticky substance to the bottoms of little drones. Then, they zoomed the drones into flowers, using the hair to pick up pollen, just like a bee does.

For now, the bee bot needs a human pilot to steer it from blossom to blossom, but scientists hope that someday, the drones could use GPS and artificial intelligence to fly all by themselves.

Other scientists are already using drones to help save endangered animals. Instead of trekking through forests or zigzagging across the ocean in boats to find and follow animals, they put robots to work for them. Drones can find, photograph, and track critters much more easily and safely than people—and they cost a fraction of the amount to operate. Scientists tracking whales in Australia used a $4,289 drone for a three-month

mission—a task that would have cost as much as $10,000 per *day* by plane. Right now, drones are following at-risk animals from koalas to migrating birds.

UP, UP, AND AWAY

On July 7, 2016, an online shopper in Cambridge, England, put a TV streaming device and a bag of popcorn into his shopping cart and clicked "order." Thirteen minutes later, a small drone touched down by his front steps, released a package, and took off into the sky again. Drone delivery is already possible—so why aren't robots bringing us our groceries?

The American Federal Aviation Administration (FAA) is facing a drone debate—some people are concerned that camera drones could be used to spy on people against their will, and others are worried that drones aren't advanced enough to fly in cities without crashing into people, buildings, or each other. So far, the technology is now only being tested in certain countries.

But many companies are convinced these hurdles won't stop drones from filling the skies. One group in Singapore hopes to fix a shortage of food service workers with drone waiters that can navigate through a crowded restaurant using infrared sensors, while carrying up to 4.4 pounds (2 kg). Another is already testing a huge drone the size of a commercial airplane meant to fly over areas that don't have Internet access, and use lasers to beam the World Wide Web to the people below. They hope this laser-powered drone will make information accessible to all seven billion people on Earth.

From saving animals at risk to serving pizza, drones that will help solve problems are in the works across the world. These flying robots aren't just the future—they're already taking off.

This "parcelcopter" drone can carry up to 2.65 pounds (1.2 kg).

microdrones.com

PACKSET

Drones like this one could help pollinate flowers someday.

INDEX

Boldface indicates illustrations.

INDEX

INDEX

CREDITS

GI: Getty Images; NGC: National Geographic Creative: NPL: Nature Picture Library; SS: Shutterstock

Cover and spine: (frog), Chris Mattison/NPL; (skeleton), Martin Dallaire/SS; (hand), Goncalo Carreira/Dreamstime; (closed treasure chest), age fotostock/Alamy Stock Photo; (open treasure chest), Agencja Fotograficzna Caro/Alamy Stock Photo; (shark fin), Digitalstormcinema/Dreamstime; (shark attacking), Mogens Trolle/SS; (page peeling back), Exclusively/SS; **back cover:** (flower) Serg64/SS; (astronaut), NASA; **Front matter:** 1, Abie Za A Ghani/EyeEm/GI; 2-3, Cody Roy/Caters News Agency; 3 (UP), stockphoto mania/SS; 4 (UP), Karl Zemlin; 4 (CTR), Anand Varma/NGC; 4 (LO), David du Plessis/Gallo Images/GI; 5 (UP), stockphoto mania/SS; 5 (CTR), Angela Bax/EyeEm/GI; 5 (LO), Ingo Arndt/Minden Pictures; **Chapter 1:** 6, jimmyjamesbond/iStockphoto; 8-9, Matt Cardy/GI; 10, Amazing Planet/Exclusive-pix; 10 (LO), Eerkia Schulz/Caters News Agency; 10 (UP RT), FLPA/REX/SS; 11 (corpse flower), Lori Epstein/NGC; 11 (CTR), Irwin Lightstone; 11 (LO), Karl Zemlin; 11 (UP), FLPA/REX/SS; 12 (LE), Science History Images/Alamy Stock Photo; 12 (RT), Carsten Peter/NGC; 12-13, Minerva Studio/SS; 13 (LO LE), Jim Reed/Corbis Documentary/GI; 13 (LO CTR), Anthony Boccaccio/NGC; 13 (UP LE), Mike Hollingshead/age fotostock/GI; 13 (UP RT), dennnis/SS; 13 (CTR), Eric Isselée/iStockPhoto; 13 (LO RT), Photodisc; 14-15, Marie-Claude Paquette/Caters News Agency; 15 (diagram), Stuart Armstrong; 16-17, Carsten Peter/NGC; 18, Alexander Ozerov/Dreamstime; 19 (LO), Paul Nicklen/NGC; 19 (UP), Stuart Armstrong; 19 (CTR), alexandre zveiger/SS; 20 (UP), Francisco Negroni/Biosphoto; 20 (LO), werner van steen/GI; 21 (UP LE), Gerry Ellis/Minden Pictures; 21 (LO), SurangaSL/SS; 21 (UP RT), Khoroshunova Olga/SS; 22-23, Kris Wiktor/SS; 23 (RT), Michael Melford/NGC; 23 (LE), Edwin L. Wisherd/NGC; 24-25, seawhisper/SS; 26, Eric Isselée/Dreamstime; **Chapter 2:** 28-29, Serg64/SS; 30-31, Paul Nicklen/NGC; 31 (diagram), Stuart Armstrong; 32-33 (octopus), Reinhard Dirscherl/SeaPics.com; 32 (UP), Bates Littlehales/NGC; 32 (LO), Jeff Rotman/NPL; 33 (CTR), Alex Mustard/NPL; 33 (LO LE), Wrangel/Dreamstime; 33 (LO RT), Constantinos Petrinos/NPL; 33 (UP), Subaqueosshutterbug/iStockphoto; 34 (LO), Cyril Ruoso/Biosphoto; 34 (UP), Mark Graf/Alamy Stock Photo; 35 (UP RT), Design Pics Inc/Alamy Stock Photo; 35 (LO), Joseph T Collins/Photo Researchers RM/GI; 35 (CTR), Bence Mate/NPL; 35 (UP LE), Kenneth C. Catania; 36-37, Jürgen Otto; 38, Francis Latreille; 39 (UP LE), Francis Latreille; 39 (UP RT), Ira Block/NGC; 39 (LO LE), Ira Block/NGC; 39 (LO RT), Francis Latreille; 40, Duncan Usher/Minden Pictures; 41 (LO), Bruce Morser/NGC; 41 (UP), Gabriel Rojo/NPL; 41 (LO), Bruce Morser/NGC; 42-43, Anand Varma/NGC; 44-45, Zoom Pet Photography/Zoom Pet Photography/GI; **Chapter 3:** 46 (LO LE), Franco Tempesta; 48-49, Jim Richardson/NGC; 50 (BOTH), Franco Tempesta; 51 (UP RT), Valentin Armianu/Dreamstime; 51 (LO), Franco Tempesta; 51 (UP LE), Royal Saskatchewan Museum; 52-53, Bettmann/GI; 53, AP Photo; 54-55, Niday Picture Library/Alamy Stock Photo; 54, Photodisc; 55 (UP RT), Niday Picture Library/Alamy Stock Photo; 55 (LO RT), Universal History Archive/UIG via GI; 55 (LO LE), Everett Historical/SS; 55 (UP LE), Courtesy of Mount Vernon Ladies' Association; 56-57, O. Louis Mazzatenta/NGC; 58-59, Franco Tempesta; 60 (LO), Carol M. Highsmith/Buyenlarge/GI; 60 (UP), World History Archive/Alamy Stock Photo; 61 (LO), PHAS/UIG via GI; 61 (UP), Universal History Archive/UIG via GI; 62, Pius Lee/SS; 63 (RT), B. Anthony Stewart/NGC; 63 (LE), Providence Pictures; 64 (UP RT), Kenneth Garrett/NGC; 64 (LO), National Maritime Museum, Greenwich, London; 64 (UP CTR), Kenneth Garrett; 64 (UP LE), Kenneth Garrett/NGC; 65 (LO LE), CM Dixon/Print Collector/GI; 65 (LO RT), Leon Neal/AFP/GI; 65 (UP LE), Romeo Gacad/AFP/GI; 65 (UP RT), Universal History Archive/UIG via GI; 65 (UP LE), CM Dixon/Print Collector/GI; **Chapter 4:** 66, Staff Sgt. Aaron D. Allmon II/U.S. Air Force photo; 68-69, Roland Seitre/Minden Pictures; 70-71, Bain Collection/Epics/GI; 70, APIC/Hulton Archive/GI; 71, Bettmann/GI; 72 (UP), Oliver Furrer/Photographer's Choice/GI; 72 (LO), Purestock/GI; 73 (UP LE), David Gowans/Alamy Stock Photo; 73 (LO), Peter Titmuss/Alamy Stock Photo; 73 (UP RT), Pat Canova/Alamy Stock Photo; 74, Georgethefourth/iStockphoto/GI; 74-75, Senior Master Sgt. Thomas Meneguin/U.S. Air Force photo; 75 (LO), Master Sgt. Val Gempis/U.S. Air Force photo; 75 (UP LE), U.S. Air Force photo; 75 (UP RT), Staff Sgt. Aaron D. Allmon II/U.S. Air Force photo; 76-77, Ghislain Simard/Biosphoto; 77 (LO), Marine2844/iStockphoto/GI; 77 (UP), Anthony Leonardo and Igor Siwanowicz, Janelia Research Campus/HHMI; 78-79, Ida Mae Astute/ABC via GI; 78, Jared Alden/Aurora Open/GI; 79 (CTR), Marcus Brandt/dpa picture alliance archiv/Alamy Stock Photo; 79 (UP), William England/Hulton Archive/GI; 79 (LO), Daniel Milchev/Stone/GI; 80 (INSET), Michael Hampshire/NGC; 80, University of Washington/NOAA/OAR/OER; 81 (LO), David Shale/NPL; 81 (UP), NOAA Okeanos Explorer Program/Science Source; 82 (LO), Christopher Swann/Biosphoto; 82 (UP), Marica van der Meer/Arterra/GI; 83 (LO), Ed Brown Wildlife/Alamy Stock Photo; 83 (UP RT), Norbert Wu/Minden Pictures; 83 (UP LE), Georgette Douwma/NPL; 84, Asher Svidensky; 85 (BOTH), David Edwards/NGC; 86-87 (Honey hunters), Andrew Newey; **Chapter 5:** 88, iurii/SS; 90-91, Mondolithic Studios; 92 (LO), NASA; 92 (UP), David Aguilar; 93 (LO), James Long & the ESA/ESO/NASA; 93 (UP RT), Dana Berry/NASA; 93 (UP LE), diversepixel/SS; 94-95, Peter Bollinger; 96-97, NASA; 98-99, Breakthrough Prize Foundation, Original artwork by Tatiana Plakhova; 99 (UP), Stuart Armstrong; 99 (LO), Kevin M. Gill; 100-103, NASA; 104-105, Mondolithic Studios; 105, Mondolithic Studios; 106-107, Mondolithic Studios; **Chapter 6:** 108, Ron Levine/The Image Bank/GI; 110-111, Jonathan Pishney/NC Museum of Natural Sciences; 111 (LE), Lenora Shell/Rob R. Dunn Lab/North Carolina State University; 111 (RT), Rob R. Dunn Lab/North Carolina State University; 112 (LO), Jurgen and Christine Sohns/Minden Pictures; 112 (UP LE), Daniel Heuclin/NPL; 112 (UP RT), Dr Edith Widder, Ocean Research & Conservation Association (ORCA); 113 (LO), Mic Clark Photography/Alamy Stock Photo; 113 (UP LE), Xavier Eichaker/Biosphoto; 113 (UP RT), Hotshotsworldwide/Dreamstime; 113 (INSET), Daniel Heuclin/NPL; 114, Sebastian Kaulitz/SS; 114-115, Derek Latta/E+/GI; 115 (UP LE), Mega Pixel/SS; 115 (LO), Nisakorn Neera/SS; 115 (CTR), Photo Melon/SS; 115 (UP RT), Oliver Hoffmann/SS; 116-117, Toshifumi Kitamura/AFP/GI; 118, Robert Clark/NGC; 119 (RT), Sebastian Kaulitzk/SS; 119 (RT), Hung Chung Chih/SS; 120, Geri Lavrov/Photographer's Choice/GI; 121 (LE), slava17/SS; 121 (RT), Hong Vo/SS; 122-123, Tony Heald/NPL; 124-125, Ishiyama & Brecht 2016; 125, Ishiyama & Brecht 2016; 126 (LO), James Cavallini/Science Source; 126 (UP), Eye of Science/Science Source; 127 (LO), Cheryl Power/Science Source; 127 (UP LE), Professors Pietro M. Motta & Tomonori Naguro/Science Source; 127 (UP RT), Dr. Jan Schmoranze/Science Source; **Chapter 7:** 128, Layland Masuda/SS; 130-131, Clark James Mishler; 132 (LO), Image Republic Inc./Alamy Stock Photo; 132 (UP), Beth Swanson/SS; 133 (CTR), Findlay/Alamy Stock Photo; 133 (UP RT), TinaFields/iStockphoto/GI; 133 (LO), Aggie 11/SS; 133 (UP LE), successo images/SS; 134-135, Comet Photography Inc.; 136, Studioportosabbia/Dreamstime; 137 (CTR), Norman Chan/SS; 137 (LO), Victor Torres/SS; 137 (UP), Olga Miltsova/SS; 138-139, JGI/Jamie Gril/Blend Images/GI; 140, Science History Images/Alamy Stock Photo; 141 (LO), xPacifica/NGC; 141 (UP), Catherine Karnow/NGC; 142 (LO), JamesChen/SS; 142 (UP LE), Roman Samokhin/SS; 142 (UP RT), M Rutherford/SS; 143 (LO LE), DElight/E+/GI; 143 (CTR), lauraslens/SS; 143 (UP), Tigergallery/SS; 143 (LO RT), billysfam/SS; 144, gerenme/iStockphoto/GI; 145 (LE), ivanastar/E+/GI; 145 (RT), Topic Images Inc./GI; 146-147, Darron R. Silva/Aurora Creative/GI; 147, Stuart Armstrong; **Chapter 8:** 148, Steve Gettle/Minden Pictures; 150-151, Stocktrek Images/NGC; 152 (UP), Corbis/SuperStock; 152 (LO), Tetra Images/GI; 153 (UP LE), Digital Vision Ltd./SuperStock; 153 (UP RT), Alessandro Bianch/Reuters; 153 (LO), U.S. Dept of the Treasury; 154-155, F1online digitale Bildagentur GmbH/Alamy Stock Photo; 156-157, NASA/Newsmakers/GI; 158, Rebecca Hale/NGC; 159 (LO), Bruce Morser/NGC; 159 (UP), Lenkadan/SS; 160 (UP), NASA, ESA, and the Hubble Heritage Team (STScI/AURA); 160 (LO), Joe McNally/NGC; 161 (LO RT), imageBROKER/Alamy Stock Photo; 161 (LO LE), Franco Tempesta; 161 (UP LE), Jirsak/SS; 161 (UP RT), NASA and G. Bacon (STScI); 162, Chien Lee/Minden Pictures; 163 (LE), Mark Moffett/Minden Pictures; 163 (RT), Martin Dohrn/NPL; 164-165, imageBROKER/Alamy Stock Photo; 165, University of Portsmouth, UK; **Chapter 9:** 166, The Atlas robot created by Boston Dynamics; 168-169, Bettmann/GI; 170 (UP), Robert Coburn/John Kobal Foundation/GI; 170 (LO), Library of Congress; 171 (UP RT), Bezmaski/Dreamstime; 171 (UP LE), Andrew Rich/E+/GI; 171 (LO), AlenKadr/SS; 172-173, Boston Dynamics; 174-175, Manfred Gottschalk/Alamy Stock Photo; 176 (UP), stockphoto-graf/SS; 176 (LO), chieferu/iStockphoto/GI; 177 (LO), itsmejust/SS; 177 (UP LE), Olekcii Mach/Alamy Stock Photo; 177 (UP RT), Dupuy Florent/SIPA/Newscom; 178, NASA; 179 (LO), NASA/JPL-Caltech; 179 (CTR), Mark Thiessen/NGC; 179 (UP), Robert Clark/NGC; 180-181, Mondolithic Studios; 182 (LO), David Buzzard/Alamy Stock Photo; 182 (UP), AG-PHOTOS/SS; 183 (UP LE), Phanie/Alamy Stock Photo; 183 (LO), GK Hart/Vikki Hart/The Image Bank/GI; 183 (UP RT), Dragon Images/SS; 184-185, Wolfgang Rattay/Reuters; 185, Eijiro Miyako, NMRI, AIST; 185 (INSET), Eijiro Miyako, NMRI, AIST; **Back matter:** 186 (shark attacking), Mogens Trolle/SS

FOR BLAKE, FELLOW LOVER OF THE WONDERFULLY WEIRD. —SWD

Since 1888, the National Geographic Society has funded more than 12,000 research, exploration, and preservation projects around the world. The Society receives funds from National Geographic Partners, LLC, funded in part by your purchase. A portion of the proceeds from this book supports this vital work. To learn more, visit natgeo.com/info.

NATIONAL GEOGRAPHIC and Yellow Border Design are trademarks of the National Geographic Society, used under license.

For more information, visit nationalgeographic.com, call 1-800-647-5463, or write to the following address:

National Geographic Partners
1145 17th Street N.W.
Washington, D.C. 20036-4688 U.S.A.

Visit us online at nationalgeographic.com/books

For librarians and teachers: ngchildrensbooks.org

More for kids from National Geographic: natgeokids.com

For information about special discounts for bulk purchases, please contact National Geographic Books Special Sales: specialsales@natgeo.com

For rights or permissions inquiries, please contact National Geographic Books
Subsidiary Rights: bookrights@natgeo.com

Designed by Fuszion

The publisher would like to thank the following people for making this book possible: Kate Hale, senior editor; Amanda Larsen, design director; Lori Epstein, director of photography; Stephanie Warren Drimmer, writer and researcher; Sally Abbey, managing editor; Joan Gossett, production editorial manager; and Gus Tello and Anne LeongSon, production assistants.

Hardcover ISBN: 978-1-4263-3183-1
Reinforced library binding ISBN:
978-1-4263-3184-8

Printed in China
18/PPS/1

SHHH...
HERE'S ONE LAST SECRET!

Sharks constantly lose and regrow their teeth. Just one shark can go through 30,000 teeth in a lifetime!